Make It with Style

WINDOW SHADES

Make It with Style
WINDOW SHADES

Donna Lang

WITH JUDY PETERSEN

PHOTOGRAPHY BY DENNIS KRUKOWSKI
ILLUSTRATIONS BY JOAN MULLIN

Clarkson Potter/Publishers
New York

With special thanks and appreciation to all the talented designers and their skilled workrooms who shared their window-dressing creations with us, and to the clients who allowed us to photograph their homes. Thank you Pam, Renato, Susan, Andrzej, Dennis, Joan, Judy, and Tiina for making your contributions to this book with such style.

Copyright © 1997 by Donna Lang

All rights reserved. No part of this book may be reproduced or transmitted in any form or by any means, electronic or mechanical, including photocopying, recording, or by any information storage and retrieval system, without permission in writing from the publisher.

Published by Clarkson N. Potter, Inc., 201 East 50th Street, New York, New York 10022. Member of the Crown Publishing Group.

Random House, Inc. New York, Toronto, London, Sydney, Auckland www.randomhouse.com

CLARKSON N. POTTER, POTTER, and colophon are trademarks of Crown Publishers, Inc.

Printed in Hong Kong

Design by Andrzej Janerka

Library of Congress Cataloging-in-Publication Data
Lang, Donna.
Make it with style : window shades : with ideas, illustrations, and instructions for Roman, Austrian, and balloon shades / by Donna Lang with Judy Petersen ; photography by Dennis Krukowski ; illustrations by Joan Mullin.—1st ed.
Includes index.
1. Window shades. 2. Blinds. I. Petersen, Judy (Judy A.). II. Title.
TT390.L3   1997   645'.3—dc21   96-49687

ISBN 0-517-88237-X

10   9   8   7   6   5   4   3

PREVIOUS PAGE: *This striking window dressing is very easy to construct using fabric with enough body to hold the crumpled look. For complete directions, see page 66.* RIGHT: *This stationary shade, also pictured on page 40, is simple to construct and has an elegant tailored look.*

Contents

Introduction

As an interior designer, I work with a host of clients each year, planning dozens of window dressings, yet each collaboration—and end result—is unique. Some people have defined tastes and know exactly what they want and why. Others know only what they don't want and are seeking suggestions on appropriate treatments. Still, all have one factor in common: The window coverings we ultimately select and create must address the needs of our rooms while satisfying our personal visions and desires.

Susan and Joel, for example, own a Tudor home with strong, well-proportioned and -positioned windows that feature graphic leaded panes. The home was landscaped to afford privacy and, not surprisingly, the couple wanted to leave the windows bare to show off their beauty.

The problem: During some points in the day, the sunlight streaming into certain rooms was simply too intense, overheating the rooms, posing potential sun damage to furniture, and creating excessive glare off the panes. And at night the windows became large black holes that made rooms appear cold and uninviting.

Semi-sheer, plain Roman shades were a perfect solution in several of the problem rooms, and did not make too bold a statement for the owners. In most cases, the inside-mounted shades could be drawn up out of sight to expose each stunning window and picturesque view. During the hours when the sun was strongest, the shade could be drawn as needed, its translucent fabric diffusing light but not shutting it out. At night the lowered shades drew the eye away from the negative empty space and added just the right touch of coziness.

Although the unembellished shades were simple in style, they effectively addressed the specific desires of the clients and the needs of the room. Susan and Joel are comfortable with adding trims to some of their Roman shades, covering formerly bare windows with cloud shades for a soft look, and installing simple panels under tailored cornices for a more streamlined effect.

The moral of the story: There is a window treatment for every situation, though choosing the right one can be a bit overwhelming. It's easiest if you first assess the "whys" of the situation, keeping in mind an inventory of your tastes and the room's dimensions, and then work through the generalities to finally be prepared to take on the specifics of the chosen designs.

Like *Make It with Style: Draperies & Swags,* this book begins with an overview of the most common reasons to consider covering your windows—from aesthetics to necessity. But I realize just knowing the reasons doesn't automatically single out the best specific design, and that's where my list of often-asked, time-tested questions is helpful. From "Do I need privacy?" to "Do I use this room mostly in the day, mostly at night, or a combination of the two?" to "How committed am I to maintaining my window dressings?," these queries are simply meant to help you assess your needs and establish priorities so you can pinpoint the best treatment for your

*Metallic organza creates a moiré pattern on this elegant Roman shade
when two layers are joined together before the shade is constructed. See page 42
for complete directions on making this shade.*

window, room, and lifestyle. The answers to these questions—and the handy Window Treatment Checklist on page 15—effectively eliminate less suitable window covering choices. Then simply choose the design you like the best!

After that all-important decision is made comes the exciting hands-on task of choosing fabric, trims, notions, and hardware. In this venture, we'll once again look at the pragmatic and aesthetic factors involved. Along the way, I'll share my behind-the-scenes knowledge, including handy reference guides and special tips, along with answers to dozens of questions such as: Which fabrics will endure direct sunlight? Does my shade need a lining? How do I miter bias binding? What are my options for mounting shades?

Then it's on to the part of the process many of us find the most stressful: measuring and estimating. However, there's really nothing to fear. Understanding the basics of measuring, learning standard allowances, and familiarizing yourself with a simple formula that can be fine-tuned to almost any shade-making situation will result in professional-looking projects.

Parts 2 and 3 of this book take you step by step through creating delightful Roman, balloon, and Austrian shades, respectively, with styles adaptable to almost any decor. In Part 4, a handy Resource Guide, beginning on page 94, offers information about where to find materials, and quick-reference glossaries define terms, fabrics, trims, and hardware specific to the shade projects.

Before You Begin

Shades are just right for so many situations, and almost all are relatively simple to make. All start with the same basic tenets but can be customized to create a unique ambience for your home. How do you decide if a shade is right for your window? Once you've reviewed this section, you'll be able to make informed decisions about your window covering's aesthetic elements, including style, fabric, and trim. Once those choices are behind you, simply bone up on the "nuts and bolts" of creating a shade, from choosing and installing window hardware, to measuring for your treatment and estimating fabric needs. Remember: Planning is key to any successful project, so take your time.

Deciding How to Dress Your Windows

1. DO I NEED PRIVACY IN THIS ROOM? If you feel as though you're in a fishbowl because of traffic passing by or because the room faces a neighbor's window, then you need a treatment (and fabric opacity) that at least offers you the *option* of privacy. However, if the window looks out onto a wooded backyard and offers you an opportunity to commune unfettered with nature, perhaps you need no dressing at all or simply one that leaves the majority of the window uncovered.

2. IS LIGHT CONTROL IMPORTANT TO THE FUNCTION OF THIS ROOM? Consider what activities are taking place at different times of the day. For instance, if you watch television in this room, you'll want window treatments that help you control the amount of light and glare on the screen. Likewise, if you're choosing window coverings for a bedroom, you'll likely want them to have a room-darkening capability in case you want to sleep when the sun doesn't.

3. HOW IMPORTANT IS LIGHT TO MY PSYCHE? Some people require more sunlight than others to remain cheerful. If you crave light and privacy isn't an issue, you may need no treatment. However, if you want the option of privacy, select a treatment that covers the window but lends itself to being made in a sheer or semi-sheer fabric that will diffuse, but not entirely block, the sun's rays.

4. WHAT STYLE AND FEELING DO I WANT TO CONVEY IN THIS ROOM? Pinpointing a style such as traditional, neoclassical, country, or romantic is usually the easy part. Then you must decide exactly how that decor can work for you to generate a feeling and mood. This translates to that enigmatic word, ambience—and this is where your own personal style really comes into play.

5. WILL BARE WINDOWS ALLOW TOO MUCH HEAT TO ESCAPE IN THE WINTER OR MAKE COOLING MY HOME DIFFICULT IN THE SUMMER? Window coverings can make a money-saving difference by offering better temperature control. In win-

ter, open them to take advantage of the sun's natural heat during the warmest part of the day, then close them as tightly as possible to keep in it; in summer, close window coverings as much as possible during the day, then open them after sundown to cool a room (both literally and visually). Choosing close-fitting treatments and adding linings and interlinings will increase your windows' energy efficiency.

PRECEDING PAGES: *The hem detail on this simple Roman shade was suggested by the patchwork of the print. See page 44 for detailed instructions.* LEFT: *Consider combining two or more design elements on your windows. Roman shades of sheer linen gauze complement printed lined and interlined drapery panels.* ABOVE: *Austrian shades can be used successfully in tailored spaces, adding softness and texture without interfering with the architectural detailing around the window.*

Shade Fast-Facts

After creating a job description for your window covering, it's time to choose a type of window shade. Shades offer so many variations that virtually *any* window challenge can be solved with an appropriate style. Want something light and airy? Use voile or lace for a translucent shade. Need a tailored statement? How about a canvas hobbled Roman shade? Is frilly and feminine in order? Create a poufy balloon shade from a romantic floral. Or combine a shade with panels and valances for a more elaborate effect (see page 76).

Shades also provide some compelling benefits:

• **AESTHETICS.** Nothing helps to assert a room's style more effectively than the perfect window dressings. Whether it's a tailored Roman shade capturing a look of streamlined modernity or an elaborate Austrian shade inspiring drama as it cascades along the length of a formal living room wall, the right combination of fabric and style will set the tone for a well-dressed room.

• **EASE.** Once you've mastered the basic concept, most shades are easy to make (though they often don't look it).

6. HOW COMMITTED AM I TO MAINTAINING MY WINDOW DRESSINGS? This answer will affect not only the window covering you choose, but also the type of fabric. (Refer to Choosing Fabric, page 17, for suggestions.) Your chosen fabric needs a cleaning method and schedule you can live with.

7. DOES THE ROOM'S FUNCTION CHANGE FROM DAY TO NIGHT? At night, undressed windows are distracting and uninviting. If you plan to spend a good deal of evening time in a room—such as a family room—it's usually best to choose window treatments that cover these "black holes" and make the room feel cozier and more protective.

8. WILL MY CHOSEN WINDOW DRESSINGS BE HIGHLY VISIBLE FROM OUTSIDE OF MY HOME? If so, pay careful attention to linings or the wrong sides of treatments: A neutral look is best.

ABOVE AND RIGHT: *Consider your window dressing in both day and nighttime light. In this room designed by the late Robert Metzger, fabric shades allow the sun in during the day but cover the dark glass at night.*

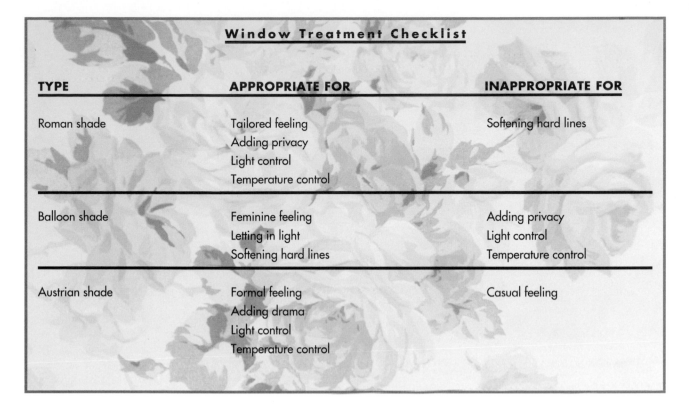

Window Treatment Checklist

TYPE	APPROPRIATE FOR	INAPPROPRIATE FOR
Roman shade	Tailored feeling Adding privacy Light control Temperature control	Softening hard lines
Balloon shade	Feminine feeling Letting in light Softening hard lines	Adding privacy Light control Temperature control
Austrian shade	Formal feeling Adding drama Light control Temperature control	Casual feeling

• ECONOMY. Since most shades use less fabric and trim yardage than curtains and draperies, you may decide to splurge on a more expensive fabric or an elaborate trim that would otherwise be out of the question.

• ENERGY EFFICIENCY. It's true! Some window shades can *save* you money by lowering your energy bill. For example, special multilayer interlining products used with close-fitting Roman shades can make a dramatic difference in the amount of heat you keep in during cold months and keep out during warmer ones.

• LIGHT CONTROL. If too much light streams in at the wrong times, choose a light-controlling treatment. Shades that can be let down are good choices, especially when they are lined and interlined to add room-darkening qualities. Unlike treatments that draw apart at the center and stack at the sides, shades also offer the inherent advantage that, when open, they concentrate at the upper window to block glare where it is typically the worst.

• PRIVACY. If you're not into elaborate window treatments but prefer privacy, shades can provide privacy with little effort. Choose an inside mount style in a lightweight fabric that pulls up to a depth of as little as 2 inches and you'll hardly know it's there—but it will be there when you need it.

• VERSATILITY. Shades can be made from virtually any fabric choice, from cotton broadcloth to silk taffeta. And width is no object for many shades, which can be pieced to almost limitless widths or divided into sections for more flexible light control. Shades also can be used where long curtain panels are impractical—where structural factors such as radiators or window seats protrude below the window—and offer both inside- and outside-mount options.

Roman, balloon, and Austrian shades all are based on similar principles and require essentially the same hardware and notions. All draw up via a network of cords strung through rings secured to the wrong side of the shade. The cords then travel to one side of the shade through screw eyes or pulleys mounted along a mounting board. All three shade types can be mounted in, on, or outside of the window frame.

This linen gauze folds beautifully into a relaxed festoon shade (directions are on page 76). Purchase a yard of your fabric choice, or borrow a large fabric memo to simulate your window treatment at home before investing in total yardage.

Choosing Fabric

For help in choosing just the right fabric, refer to the Fiber Wear and Care chart on page 20 and the following guidelines, which comprise my personal checklist for choosing fabric:

• Don't skimp. If your budget is tight, it's better to use unbleached muslin luxuriously than expensive silk sparingly.

• Don't forget that your time or your labor bill (if you're using a custom workroom or dressmaker) will be the same whether you choose beautiful fabric or a disappointing substitute.

• If you're considering a patterned fabric for a shade or other treatment that will be drawn, shirred, or pleated, gather it together in your hand (horizontally for Roman shades, and both horizontally and vertically for balloon and Austrian shades) to see how it will look at the window. Many designs look beautiful flat, but look too busy or lose their impact when manipulated.

• When windows should not be accented—such as when window placement or proportion is a prob-

lem or when the emphasis should go to other more important elements in the room—choose a fabric to match or to blend with the wall color and value.

• When the windows should be the primary focal point, such as in a room with high ceilings and elegantly proportioned windows, choose dramatic fabrics (and trims), then reflect them in the room's other furnishings.

• Keep in mind the type of light exposure your window dressings will receive. Natural fibers such as silk, linen, and cotton will eventually rot in direct sunlight, although appropriate linings can effectively lengthen their lives.

• Before purchasing the total yardage for your window coverings, buy just one yard and live with it for a few days. Viewing it at different times of the day—and with other fabrics in the room—can help you decide if you're willing to commit to it.

• Always check the manufacturer's labels for information about cleaning your fabric. When in doubt, consult a reputable dry cleaner for advice.

Lining and Interlining

Linings can add opacity, drape, and elegance to Roman and balloon shades (Austrian shades generally are not lined). To add further softness, body, and depth to lined Roman shades, also add a flannel interlining (refer to Part 2 for specifics). Unless otherwise specified to accommodate a variation, follow these lining tips:

• **Cut size.** Cut the lining for a basic Roman or balloon shade slightly narrower than the shade face fabric (2 to 4 inches, depending on the treatment; after pleating for balloon shades) and the same length. When the shade edges are bound, the lining is cut the same size as the face fabric.

• **Seaming.** Seam the panels of lining fabric as you would panels of face fabric. Plan any lining and face fabric seams so they coincide with the ring positions.

• **Hemming.** This will vary greatly, depending on the shaping, embellishment, and weighting of the lower edge.

As an example, on a basic Roman shade, you'll create a rod pocket for a weight bar (used to help the shade hang straight and taut) in the first turn of the doubled hem, then finish both the face fabric and lining separately with 4-inch doubled hems. On a pleated balloon shade, you'll position the lining lower edge 2 inches above the face fabric lower edge, then encase it in the face fabric's 1-inch doubled hem; this hem also will serve as the weight bar rod pocket.

• **Construction.** For both basic Roman and balloon shades, seam the lining and face fabrics right-sides-together, positioning as noted for the specific treatment; when turned and pressed, the face fabric will frame the lining side edges. On bound-edge treatments, however, the face fabric and lining may simply be placed wrong-sides-together before binding. Frequently, linings will be cut slightly longer than necessary, then trimmed at the shade upper edge after fitting.

Trim Options

The icing on the cake, trims often are what separate the ordinary from the extraordinary. (For an overview of trim types, refer to the Decorative Trims glossary on page 91.) Trims add detail and luxury, define shapes, and reiterate a design style in a room. That's why your trim selection can be just as important as your fabric choice—and subject to the same emotional response. My advice? Follow your heart, tempered when needed by the realities of your room, windows, and budget. These guidelines should help:

• Balance the decoration of your windows with the detail in the room. Use simple trims like twill tape, ribbon, flat braid, small-scale piping, or a single ruffle for wonderful (usually affordable) impact on dressings in uncluttered or contemporary spaces. In contrast, select generous tassels, fringe of all kinds, large-scale piping, multiple ruffles, and other more elaborate trims to create a stunning effect on treatments in elaborate, formal, or period rooms (for an example of use of fringe, refer to the Festoon Shade on page 76).

• Use your trims to your best advantage. If you want to emphasize a desired color in a print, purchase trim in that color. If you want your treatments to echo a certain period, choose embellishments that underscore the point.

• Seek out trims in unlikely places. Fine trims often outlast the treatments they adorn, so consider saving the fringe, braid, or tassels from old curtains and reusing them on new window dressings. Or scout trims still in good condition on draperies at thrift and consignment shops or auctions. Often you can purchase the whole drapery for much less than the trim alone would cost!

For additional information on applying and creating trims to decorate shades, refer to Part 4: Tools, Terms, and Techniques.

Where to Apply Trim

Although personal preference usually is the best guide to where trims should be applied, you may find these general suggestions helpful for choosing the most eye-pleasing placements:

• **BAND TRIMS.** Ribbon, gimp, middy braid, rickrack, and other flat trims usually look best set in from the edge they are to embellish—the wider the band, the greater the distance you should allow between the trim and the fabric edge. For example, a 1-inch-wide band trim often looks attractive set in ½ inch from the edge of a Roman shade, while a 2-inch-wide band trim usually looks best 1 inch from the same edge.

• **FRINGE.** Most fringe types lend themselves to one of two placements: with the heading lower edge even with the treatment edge or with the entire heading set in from the edge so the lower edge of the fringe aligns with the treatment edge. It's best to experiment by holding the trim in both locations before making a final decision. Fringe is usually applied only at the lower edge of shades. Crowding fringe as you sew or using a double layer (choose two different colors for a wonderful custom look) will enhance the appearance of sparse or flat varieties.

• **CORD OR CORD WITH LIP.** Cord may be hand stitched or glued in place anywhere it is aesthetically pleasing: at the treatment edge, along a ruffle upper edge, or along a gathered area, to name a few. Cord with lip—that is, cord with a flat braidlike band attached—is designed for inserting in seams, such as at a treatment edge or for accenting band edges, and may be used in tandem with other inserts, such as ruffles.

Experiment with decorative trim placement on your shades, judging the best position for band trims and fringes. Balance the width of the band trim with the distance inset from the treatment edge. Fringes may extend below the edge or be set so that the bottom edge of the fringe aligns with the edge of the fabric. Another option is creating your own trims with fabric, which can be economical and stylish. Refer to Working with Trims on page 83.

Fiber Wear and Care

FIBER	WEAVES	CHARACTERISTICS	TRADITIONAL CARE	CURRENT OPTIONS
Cotton	Batiste, voile, gauze, lace Broadcloth, chintz, damask, seersucker Denim, canvas, corduroy, velveteen	Strong, absorbent, cool	Machine wash, tumble dry, or dry-clean	Crinkled and wrinkled
Linen	Sheer handkerchief weights to coarse weaves	Strong, absorbent, naturally lustrous, good dimensional stability, subject to shrinkage and wrinkles	Dry-clean, iron while damp	Hand or machine wash for deliberate wrinkles
Wool	Voile, flannel, plaids, checks, tweeds	Warm, absorbent, wrinkle resistant, subject to shrinkage	Dry-clean	Machine wash (washable woolens)
Silk	Pongee, linen, taffeta, "crunchy tweeds"	Lustrous, stable, absorbent, drapes beautifully, subject to damage from sunlight	Dry-clean or hand wash, iron while damp	Machine wash in cold water, wring and twist, tie with cord, tumble-dry low
Polyester	Alone or in combination with cotton-, silk-, wool-like blends	Strong, resists abrasion and wrinkles, subject to pill, stains, and static cling	Machine wash, iron at low temperature	Machine wash, tumble-dry
Nylon	Sheers, parachute cloth, cire, velvet	Strong, lightweight, resilient, subject to pill and static cling, fades in direct sunlight	Hand or machine wash, iron at low temperature	Machine wash, tumble-dry

Making Shades

The sewing techniques for the construction of a Roman, balloon, or Austrian shade will vary with the particular project, but the marking of the shade for ring placement and the attachment of those rings is similar for all three styles.

• **MARKING.** Marking ring or ring tape placement is one of the most important steps in ensuring your shade's success. Always start by planning your shade's ring placements on paper, taking into account the weight of the fabric and the width of the shade (the heavier and the wider, the more vertical rows required) and any piecing seams to be aligned with tapes or rings. For the best results, align the shade on a gridded cutting surface and use its markings—plus a long yardstick or other straightedge and an air-soluble marker or chalk—to mark the appropriate horizontal and vertical lines. Then mark an *x* wherever the lines intersect to designate a ring position. It is critical that the rings be even and parallel; otherwise the shade may pull or hang unevenly.

Unless specifically noted otherwise for a shade variation, position the lowermost row of rings at the upper edge of the weight bar and the uppermost row of rings 3 inches or more below the upper edge of the finished shade (mounting board front edge). The position of vertical rows will vary with the shade style, but the rings should be at least 1 inch in from the shade's side edges. Vertical row spacing generally varies between 8 and 18 inches and will depend on the shade's total width, any seams to be hidden, and the weight of the chosen fabric; as a rule of thumb, horizontal rows usually are spaced from 5 to 8 inches apart, depending on the desired pleat depth.

• **RINGS VERSUS RING TAPE.** To achieve the most professional finish, attach each ring separately. Individual rings do take time to attach, but the extra effort means that the rings are as innocuous as possible. Purchased shade tape saves time, but stitching lines show on the right side of the shade and the tape itself may show through the face fabric. Because the twill tape to which the rings are sewn has a tendency to shift position and stretch as you sew, use basting tape down the center of the shade tape to hold it in position while you sew. Self-made tapes are especially labor intensive, but they can be customized to create an eye-pleasing wrong side of the shade.

Sheer Austrian shades (see also page 72) combine beautifully with curtain panels.

Mounting and Rigging

Roman, balloon, and Austrian shades usually are hung from a mounting board but occasionally are installed on a curtain rod (usually in tandem with a mounting board) using some special notions and hardware. Window hardware mounting is a task for which the old adage "An ounce of prevention is worth of pound of cure" certainly holds true. To prevent the need for "curing" mistakes, carefully assess the window and desired design, then answer these helpful questions, *before* you begin:

1. WHERE SHOULD MY TREATMENT BE MOUNTED? Shades can be mounted inside of the window frame or outside of it, either on or above the frame. Inside-mounted shades are ideal for showing off nicely framed windows and should not extend below the sill; outside-mounted shades will

at least partially camouflage window frames and can end at the sill, at the apron lower edge, and even at the floor. All outside-mounted window coverings must project from the wall far enough to clear the window frame (if not frame-mounted) or any accompanying under-treatment such as mini-blinds or pleated shades.

2. WHERE DO I INSTALL THE HARDWARE? To determine the location of studs, lightly tap on the wall with your hammer to listen for these solid-sounding areas or use a stud-finder tool, available at your local hardware store. If you can secure basic screws into wood studs, you probably won't need any additional hardware, unless the treatment is unusually heavy.

If you can't secure the hardware into wall studs

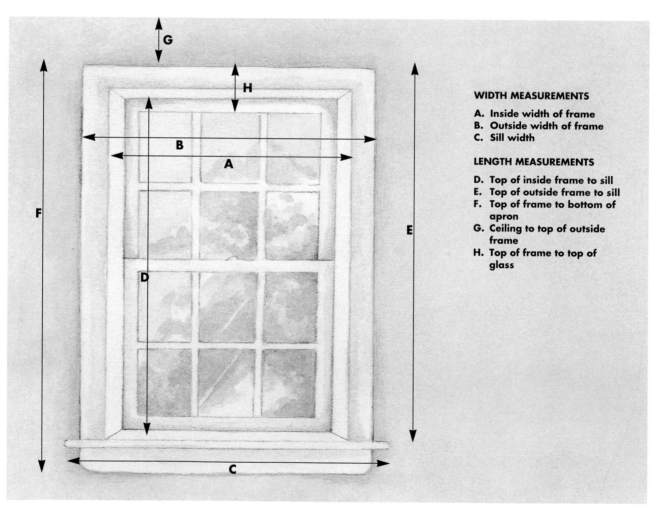

WIDTH MEASUREMENTS

A. Inside width of frame
B. Outside width of frame
C. Sill width

LENGTH MEASUREMENTS

D. Top of inside frame to sill
E. Top of outside frame to sill
F. Top of frame to bottom of apron
G. Ceiling to top of outside frame
H. Top of frame to top of glass

or a support of any kind, you'll need anchoring hardware specifically designed for this task. Called expanding hollow wall fasteners, they're designed to be inserted into predrilled holes, then tightened until they expand inside of the wall, adding strength and stability. You'll find a variety of sizes and types at your local hardware store. If the wall in question is solid plaster, concrete, or brick, you'll need a drill and appropriate bits for drilling holes for the supplied screws, plus expanding plastic plugs of an appropriate size for a snug fit.

When you're installing a mounting board, curtain rod, or board-and-rod combination, the following special tips and tricks can make a difference:

• To facilitate rigging, shades may be attached to the hardware *before* mounting to the wall or window frame. An exception to that would be if a rod-mounted shade's screw eyes are inserted directly into the window frame.

• To prepare for mounting, sketch your window on paper and mark all of the pertinent measurements on that sketch (as shown on the facing page).

• Before you begin your installation, gather together any of the following tools that apply: pencil, metal tape measure, carpenter's level, drill and assorted drill bits, screwdriver (electric varieties are easy to use and save time and stress), hammer, starter nails, partner for assisting you, and instructions included with the hardware (if any).

• Do not begin marking or drilling anything until you have planned the installation and checked that you have all of the necessary materials.

• Before you begin mounting any hardware, be sure the wall is in good repair and that all holes from previous mountings are filled with spackle and camouflaged or sanded down.

• Keep in mind that windows aren't always completely square and that floors and ceilings can be uneven. When determining your hardware height for outside mounts, always measure at each end of a window's upper edge, and at several points in between, from the mounting point to the desired length. When in doubt, mount your hardware so it is visually pleasing—such as parallel with the ceiling line—even if that means your board or rod won't be exactly level. If you are working on a shade with companion floor-

---

The Ring Thing

To apply shade rings or ring tape to the shade's wrong side or lining side, follow these basic instructions:

• **Individual rings.** Sew on individual rings by hand through all layers, positioning their upper edge over the x positions, or machine stitch them using a wide-width zigzag set to stitch in place (0 stitches per inch); stitch over the ring with 8 to 10 stitches, then lock off the stitches by stitching in place several times at each end of the zigzag. To save time, do not clip the thread between rings after sewing all the rings.

Important! Because a shade's lowermost horizontal row of rings carries the bulk of the shade's weight when drawn up, always reinforce the rings in that row with extra stitches.

• **Self tapes.** To make your own tapes (appropriate for unlined shades), cut 2-inch-wide fabric strips from the face fabric and press the long edges in to meet at the center. Stitch the rings to the strips at the determined intervals as described above for individual ring attachment. Edgestitch the tapes in place on the shade's wrong side as you would a purchased tape.

• **Purchased tapes.** To apply premade ring shade tape, preshrink it before applying, then edgestitch it in place. Or for a less obtrusive application, glue the tape in place with fabric glue and secure each ring with machine zigzag stitches as described above for individual rings.

---

length panels, hem them so they're an even distance from the floor, even if the floor isn't level.

• Check that your hardware is positioned as planned by installing only the uppermost screw in the brackets or angle irons first, then test-inserting the board or rod. If everything is in order, complete the installation. If it isn't, you'll have less to undo to correct any problem.

• If your shade has no return, conceal the treatment's screw eyes and cord rigging with a self-fabric, self-lined board end cover. See Making Mounting Board End covers on page 82.

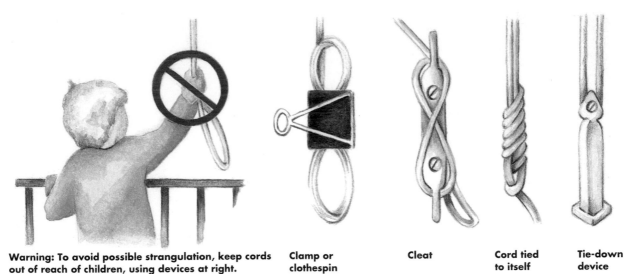

Warning: To avoid possible strangulation, keep cords out of reach of children, using devices at right.   **Clamp or clothespin**   **Cleat**   **Cord tied to itself**   **Tie-down device**

• For a neat finish at a shade's upper edge, especially on tailored shades, glue or staple a self-fabric welting strip along the front and return edge of the board.

• Remember that cords can be a source of danger to small children. Always keep cords well secured at a height that is out of their reach (see above).

The mounting and rigging process for Roman, balloon, and Austrian shades is usually identical; it is the shade construction that creates widely varied effects.

Binding the top and sides of this soft Roman shade with bias bands of the shade stripe define the silhouette atop wooden shutters.

Mounting

Shades can be hung on a mounting board using either a staple attachment or hook-and-loop tape fasteners. Occasionally, shades also are hung from a curtain rod or rod-and-mounting-board combination:

• **STAPLED ATTACHMENT.** Align the top front edge of the board with the finished shade's upper edge marks and staple the mounting board allowance to the top of the mounting board.

• **HOOK-AND-LOOP TAPE FASTENER ATTACHMENT.** Staple, glue, or tack the hook side of the fastener to the mounting board top about ½ inch in from the board's back edge. Sew the loop side to

---

Hardware and Notions Checklist

The following hardware items and related notions are the most commonly used for Roman, balloon, and Austrian shades. Refer to this list when creating the projects in Parts 2 and 3. If you're unfamiliar with any of the terms used, refer to the Hardware and Notions glossary beginning on page 90.
- Mounting board and angle irons
- Screw eyes
- Small plastic rings or shade tape designed for desired application
- Shade cord
- Cord drop

- Awning cleat
- Weight bar
- Staples and staple gun or hook-and-loop fastening tape

Note: Using a made-to-order shade lift system will eliminate the need for a number of the above supplies and is especially helpful on large, heavy shades. The system is a manually operated clutch mechanism that raises and lowers the shade via continuous-lift cords or tapes, allowing you to position the shade easily and smoothly at any height (see Resource Guide for a mail-order source).

the wrong side of the shade mounting allowance ½ inch from the shade's upper edge. If you've used a shirring tape with woven-in loop fastener, attach the corresponding hook portion to the narrow front and side edges of the board.

• **CURTAIN ROD MOUNTING.** With this type of mount, you'll create a rod pocket at the shade's upper edge, into which the curtain rod will be inserted. To mount the treatment, attach the rod to an unfinished board wide enough to accommodate the rod bracket. Paint the board the same color as the wall color, then mount the board's widest side to the wall and insert the screw eyes into the board thickness at the lower edge. When you attach the board to the wall, allow a 1-inch space between the top of the window and the board to allow room for the screw eyes. Other alternatives: Mount the rod directly to the wall and use a separate board for the screw eyes, or screw the eyes directly into the window frame.

Rigging

Rigging will follow the same basic steps for any of the three shade types. However, in some cases, you'll have to mount the board to the wall or window frame *before* attaching the shade. Following are instructions for a shade attached to the board before the board is mounted:

1. Insert the screw eyes into the board bottom, directly above each vertical row of rings sewn to the shade wrong (or lining) side. If the last screw eye is positioned more than 2 inches in from the shade edge, add an extra screw eye ½ inch in from the board end so the cords will hang near the shade's side edge.

2. Cut a shade cord the necessary length for each vertical row of rings (each will be different), based on the distance it will travel from the shade lower to upper edge and across the shade (through the screw eyes), allowing enough excess so it can be easily grasped and tied. The excess cord should be at least 18 inches or one half the window height. Refer to your paper plan to help determine the amount of cord required for stringing the shade. Traditionally, cords hang down the right side of the shade, but exceptions should be made when the right side is less accessible than the left.

3. Beginning with the vertical row of rings farthest from the side from which the shade will be pulled, tie one end of each corresponding cord to the lowermost ring on the shade, making several knots, then dab the knot area with glue. If the cord is nylon, seal the cord end with the flame of a match or a dab of glue to prevent fraying. Thread each cord up through its vertical row of rings, then horizontally through any applicable screw eyes.

4. Mount the board and attached shade at the desired position using angle irons. With the shade lowered, adjust the cords so they draw up evenly. Knot the cords together just below the end screw eye (closest to the pull-cord ends). Braid the loose cords and secure the ends together with tape. Thread the end through the cord drop, knot the cords, and trim away the excess. Attach the awning cleat to the pull-cord side of the window at a height out of reach of children.

5. To dress the shade, pull it up, arranging the folds or poufs. Loop the cord on the cleat to hold the shade in the "up" position. At each row of rings, pull and shape the folds so that they lie smoothly one on top of the other. For Roman-style shades, steam or use fabric dressing on the shade, both front and back. Lightly crease or arrange the fabric with your hands to help set the folds. Let the shade dry thoroughly. For balloon and Austrian shades, evenly distribute the fullness in the balloon sections by fanfolding the fabric with your fingers. If your fabric needs assistance to maintain the billowing effect in the poufs, fill each pouf with scrunched-up nylon net or dry cleaner plastic bags. If you plan to raise and lower the shade on a regular basis, just fill the permanent poufs at the bottom.

Measuring and Estimating

Measuring and estimating is one of the most important aspects of making a one-of-a-kind window shade. Why? Your accuracy at this point will affect the rest of the project, so it's all the more important to employ some more tried-and-true tricks of the trade. To assist you in the measuring and estimating process, refer to the illustration on page 22.

• Start with these three indispensable tools: a spring-return steel tape measure 16 to 25 feet long; a notebook and pencil for drawing window likenesses and recording measurements; and a 25-foot length of nylon cord and some pushpins for reaching, bending, and staying where a tape measure can't or for gauging a treatment's length, a scallop's dip, or any other feature.

• Measure everything twice with a partner, the first time with one of you measuring and the other writing, the second time swapping roles. There are usually subtle nuances with every custom window covering, so take time to sketch and visualize each treatment carefully, making notes and measurements of all thoughts and details. Keep in mind that identical-looking windows may not measure identically—so measure each one separately.

• When measuring for inside-mounted shades, measure the inside frame width at the top and bottom (windows may not be exactly square), choosing the narrower of the two for the shade's finished width, and the inside frame length for the finished length.

• When measuring for outside-mounted shades, measure the width of the area you wish to cover, planning to extend your treatment ½ inch but no more than 1 inch beyond the outside frame width. For frame-mounted shades on windows with sills, plan the finished width to be equal to the sill length (span across the window). The length of any outside-mounted shade will depend on your preference, the shade type and formality, and the room's needs.

• Note and measure any special considerations, such as unusual molding or sill depth, outside-mounted blinds, or wall mounting space available. These will influence both the mounting board depth and the shade mounting board allowance.

• Remember that no two design estimations are exactly alike, so don't assume that because you've made this treatment before, the yardage requirements are the same. A different fabric may mean a different construction method, different fabric layout, and different yardage requirement.

• When making multiple coverings from the same fabric(s), determine if you can conserve yardage by using the "leftovers" from each treatment.

• If you're using a print fabric with an obvious motif, plan for matching vertical and horizontal pattern repeats across the treatment.

• Think about pattern placement. For example, does your fabric have a large motif that should be centered on each balloon shade scallop?

• Think creatively by playing "What if?"—ask thought-provoking questions, such as "Can I 'edit' or cut the fabric for possible trim use?" The answer might be that you can position a pattern's stripe along a Roman shade's lower edge to create a natural border or cut the fabric on the bias to make a dynamic bound edge.

Calculating Yardage

To determine the yardage requirements for any shade, you must first select the mounting to be used and determine your shade's finished width and length (see page 27 for help with taking appropriate measurements and determining the desired finished dimensions). Once these factors are known, determining yardage may be done simply by using the following formula and adding the appropriate allowances for fullness, mounting, hems, pleats, etc.

Although this may look like an exercise in plugging in figures, it's important that you understand how the basic yardage formula works so you can effectively make allowances for special details and matches. And don't forget the most important tip of all: When in doubt, round up!

Basic Yardage Formula

1. Determine the desired finished length of the treatment and add to it any upper edge allowance (such as for board mounting) or lower edge allowance (such as for hems, special shaping on a Roman shade, or extra poufing on a balloon shade); plus any tuck allowance multiplied by the number of tucks (such as for a hobbled Roman shade); or fullness allowance (such as for an Austrian shade). If you're using a print fabric, also calculate any extra yardage required for matching or positioning prints. This will be the panel cut length.

2. Determine the desired finished width of the treatment, multiply it by the desired fullness, if any (such as for a cloud shade), and add any return (for outside mounts), pleats (such as for a basic balloon shade), ease (such as for an Austrian shade), and side hem allowances. If you're using a print or if piecing is required to create the necessary width, also calculate any extra yardage required for positioning or seaming. This will be the panel cut width.

3. Divide the panel cut width by your fabric's width (45 inches, 54 inches, 60 inches, etc.) and round up to the next whole number. This will be the number of fabric widths needed.

4. Multiply the panel cut length by the number of fabric widths needed to calculate the total fabric length in inches.

5. Divide this fabric length by 36 inches (the number of inches in a yard) to determine the total yards needed.

Details and Extra Allowances

The design details of each shade variation will require special allowances to be added to the finished shade dimensions. Use the guidelines in the Basics sections of Parts 2 and 3 as jumping-off points, then carefully document what you plan so you'll remember when it's time to sew.

To determine trim yardages for any window dressing, first calculate your treatment dimensions. Mark those measurements on a sketch of your completed window treatment with the trim areas highlighted, then add together all edges to be treated, adding extra as needed for fullness factors, mitering, and finishing ends.

This window combines an upholstered cornice (see page 82) with the pleated balloon shade featured on page 74.

Perfect Placement

When choosing a fabric with an obvious print or design, think about its placement potential on your chosen style. Ask what is the focal point on this shade; and what it will take to position a full repeat there; and how trim placement will affect the motif positioning. Then consider whether the placement you desire is possible and, if a factor, economical. Also remember that all like treatments in the same area should feature the same pattern placement. To avoid problems, map out your design on paper first and/or lay out your fabric and physically manipulate it to mock up the placement of the fabric pattern.

While some pattern placement decisions are based purely on personal preference, others come with guidelines:

• **Roman shades.** The upper portion is the most important on these shades. Position the upper edge of a vertical pattern repeat at the treatment upper edge, allowing room above it for a mounting allowance. Also center horizontal repeats from side to side; you do not want one side hem of the shade to be positioned at the center of a motif and the other positioned at the edge of the motif. Also, always position seams on both the face fabric and the lining over a row of rings.

• **Balloon and Austrian shades.** These follow the same rules as Roman shades, but horizontal repeats are especially important. Always position large motifs centered in each scallop and plan seams on pieced-width shades (and their linings, if applicable) so they will fall between scallops to be hidden in pleats or gathers.

2
Creating Roman Shades
Basics, Patterns, and Instructions

For a given window size, Roman-style shades usually require the least amount of fabric of the three basic shade styles addressed in this book, yet they can offer as much or as little privacy as you desire. In fact, a Roman shade can change its persona to adapt to almost any situation and any decorating style simply by changing fabrics and, if appropriate, trims.

For example, to create a rustic effect, choose a high-texture fabric such as burlap and accent with jute trims or twine tie-ups. For a more formal statement, select the same fabric used for panels and a valance—or a coordinating solid or print—to make a companion Roman shade, shaping the lower edge and embellishing it with braid. For barely-there shades with an eclectic appeal, choose a sheer fabric and nix the lining, as shown in the photo at left.

Roman Shade Basics

In its fully extended state, this tailored treatment usually has no vertical or horizontal fullness, although it may feature a series of horizontal tucks, such as on the hobbled variation (refer to the Hobbled Roman Shade on page 48). When drawn up, the shade layers into graceful crosswise folds, creating a look just right in so many rooms. And while Roman shades may look complicated, they're really quite basic. After you've worked through one, every one thereafter will be a breeze! When making your Roman shades, keep in mind these tips:

• **FABRICS.** As previously noted, Roman shades lend themselves to a wide range of fabrics. To help you choose the one right for your personal taste, decor, and preferred care methods, refer to Choosing Fabric (page 17) and to the Fiber Wear and Care chart (page 20).

• **LINING.** Roman shades usually are lined, unless made in a sheer or lace fabric, to improve the way they hang and their appearance from the outside. Although lining applications will vary from treatment to treatment, for many Roman-style shades, the lining will be cut slightly narrower and the same length as the face fabric and seamed to the face fabric with right sides together (refer to the Simple Roman Shade instructions on page 34).

However, there are exceptions, such as when a treatment is bound at the edge; in this case, the lining and face fabric are cut the same size and placed with wrong sides together before the edges are bound (refer to the Banded Roman Shade instructions on page 38).

• **INTERLINING.** Some Roman shades also are interlined to soften their lines or add energy efficiency. If keeping out the cold or keeping in the cool is high on your agenda (or budget), Roman shades are particularly suited for use with special multilayer

PRECEDING PAGES: *Roman shades were the ideal solution for a trio of extremely tall windows above the heating and air conditioning system. Because privacy was not an issue in this elegant living room, double-layered sheer metallic organza added a subtle shimmer during the day and softened the black rectangles created at night.*

interlinings designed for this purpose. Also available are special magnetic side rails that help keep the shade secured to the window frame for insulative purposes (see the Resource Guide on page 94 for a mail-order source).

To add an interlining to most treatments, cut and, if necessary, piece it to the same size as the fabric, then baste it to the face fabric within the hem allowances, trimming away any excess interlining beyond the basting; treat the two layers as one during construction. When you must seam interlining panels to create the necessary shade width, overlap their side edges ½ inch and sew along the overlap center with a wide zigzag stitch.

• **MEASURING.** Always measure each window carefully, double-checking each measurement to avoid accidentally sabotaging your project before you begin. Refer to Measuring and Estimating (page 27) for specific guidelines.

• **ESTIMATING YARDAGE.** Although every Roman shade (indeed every window treatment in general) will have its own subtleties and special allowances, the Basic Yardage Formula on page 28 will get you started. In addition, use as a guideline the allowances noted in the Simple Roman Shade project on page 34. To determine allowances for Roman shade variations, refer to the instructions with each project.

• **WEIGHT ROD.** Every Roman shade needs a weighted rod or slat to keep the shade aligned and its folds crisp, while adding weight and stability to the shade's lower edge. Some shades have a rod pocket built into the hem area for the bar while others hold the rod in place by tacking it just below the bottom row of rings or sometimes by way of loops made with the end of shade tapes. In the latter cases, the bar is covered in a fabric casing to allow it to be tacked to the rings or to the loops. The rod is generally a ⅜-inch solid metal rod, available through drapery supply shops and hardware stores, but a wooden dowel or a length of curtain rod sometimes is substituted.

• **DECORATIVE HEMS.** Roman shades graciously lend themselves to decorative hems that extend

Directions for this banded Roman shade are on page 38.

below the weight bar and rod pocket. These hem "extensions" are shaped and/or trimmed to echo or reinforce the overall design sensibility of a room. For example, shape the lower edge in scallops to create a soft, feminine look in a powder room, or create points accented with tassels to echo sharper lines in a masculine den.

For a basic shade hem, allow the distance between the horizontal rows of rings (to be folded in half for the hem). However, if you want a decorative hem—such as scallop, ribbon trim, or border edging—you will need a deeper hem allowance. For more information on creating decorative hems, see page 44.

• **HARDWARE AND MOUNTING.** Roman shades may be inside- or outside-mounted. For details on all of the hardware and notions required, plus mounting tips and tricks, refer to Making Shades (page 21) and the Hardware and Notions Checklist (page 25). Also refer to the specific instructions for the treatments featured here in Part 2.

• **DRESSING.** Pull the shade up, arranging the folds. Loop the cord on the cleat to hold the shape in the "up" position. At each row of rings, pull and shape the folds so that they lie smoothly one on top of the other. Steam or use fabric dressing on the shade, both front and back. Lightly crease or arrange the fabric with your hands to help set the folds. Let the shade dry thoroughly.

• **MAINTENANCE.** To keep your Roman shades looking good, lightly vacuum them every month. Or for treatments without delicate trims, carefully remove them from their mountings (hook-and-loop tape attachments make this easy), remove their cords and weight bar, and air-fluff them in the dryer. When it's time for cleaning, again carefully remove them from their mountings and remove their cords and bar, then follow the method prescribed for your fabric (dry cleaning is usually recommended).

SIMPLE ROMAN SHADE

*Master this basic construction to create a variety of shades, from lined, unlined,
or layered to room-darkening interpretations.*

SEWING INSTRUCTIONS
Constructing the Shade

1. On the face fabric, press up (do not sew) a 5-inch double hem. (If you want to give your hem some additional body, cut a piece of buckram or fleece batting to the finished width of the shade by $3/8$ inch less than the depth of the hem and insert in hem area.) On the lining fabric, press up 5 inches and stitch across the hem $1\frac{1}{2}$ inches from the hem fold, making a rod pocket. Fold the lining up another 5 inches and press and pin to make a 5-inch double hem.

2. With right sides together, place the lining so that the bottom of its hem is $\frac{1}{4}$ inch above the hem edge of the face fabric. Match the side edges, pin, and sew together with $\frac{1}{2}$-inch seams, leaving the top edges open.

3. Lay out the shade with the lining side up. Make a small slit, $\frac{3}{4}$ inch wide, at one end of the rod pocket, cutting through the top layer of lining only. The rod will be inserted here later.

4. Turn the shade right side out, center the lining on the face fabric, and press. The lining is narrower than the face fabric, so $\frac{1}{2}$ inch of face fabric will extend to the lining side of the shade.

MATERIALS
* See Hardware and Notions Checklist, page 25.

YARDAGE AND CUTTING

1. The cut width of the shade face fabric is equal to the finished width of the shade plus 2 inches for side hems. The lining is cut without the 2-inch hem allowance.

2. The cut length of the face *and* lining fabrics is the finished length, plus mounting board allowance, and 11 inches for hems.

3. Alter the hem allowance, if necesssary, to accommodate deeper or shallower folds, or to change the amount of hem that shows below the first fold. See Step 2 under Planning and Sewing Rings, opposite, for more details.

5. From the lining side, stitch the bottom hems in place $4\frac{3}{4}$ inches up from the bottom edge of the face fabric.

6. On the lining side of the shade, measure up from the hem edge and mark the finished length of the shade. Measure $1\frac{3}{4}$ inches (or the depth of the board) from this line toward the raw edge at the top of the shade; trim off the excess fabric and lining. Clean-finish the raw edges with a serger or zigzag stitch.

Planning and Sewing Rings

1. On the lining side of the shade, use a yardstick to mark the vertical lines where the rings will be placed, keeping them even and parallel. The outermost lines should be 1 inch in from the edge; the rows in between should be spaced evenly, 8 to 12 inches apart. It is very important for rings, cords, and screw eyes to be perfectly aligned.

2. Mark the ring positions along the vertical lines, placing the first ring at the bottom, just above the rod pocket. The last ring at the top must be 3 inches or more down from the top finished line of the shade. Make the rings between 6 inches apart. For shallower or deeper folds, adjust the ring spacing. All the rings must align perfectly across the shade (right).

3. Sew the rings to the lining side at the marked spots, by hand or machine zigzag stitch, using thread that matches the face fabric and catching a tiny amount of the face fabric as you sew. (To sew rings on by machine, use a zigzag stitch and lower the feed dogs; cover rings with 8 to 10 stitches. You can move from one ring spot to the next without cutting threads.)

4. Turn out the bottom hem to expose the rod pocket. Cut a weight rod 1¼ inches shorter than the finished width of the shade and insert it through the slit. Stitch the slit closed and turn the hem down again.

5. Mount, rig, and dress the shade according to the instructions on pages 22 to 26.

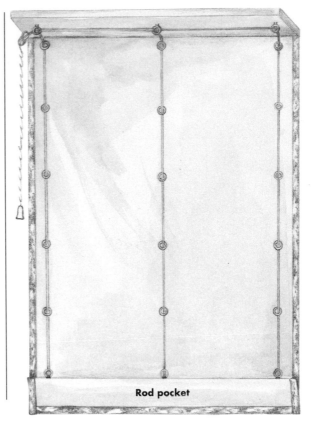

Rod pocket

Mitering Flat Trims

Ribbons, braids, and other flat trims with two finished edges often are used to create borders on flat treatments such as Roman shades—and that can require turning corners. The best way to do this is to miter the corner, which means you'll need a little extra trim (an amount equal to the trim width for each corner). Always begin by marking the trim placement lines as noted earlier. The following instructions are for trims with two straight edges; for trims with one straight and one decorative edge, position the straight edge on the placement line and edgestitch only that edge.

1. Position the outer trim edge along the placement line and edgestitch each edge up to 2 inches from the placement line corner intersection.

2. Fold the trim back onto itself at the placement line corner and draw a 45-degree angle from the outer corner

to the inner corner; pin along the angle.

3. Fold down the trim to check the angle (the trim should align with the adjacent placement line). Lift the trim back up, remove the pin(s), and stitch the diagonal line.

4. If the trim is bulky, trim the corner close to the stitching.

5. Reposition the trim edge on the adjacent line and continue stitching the trim on that line.

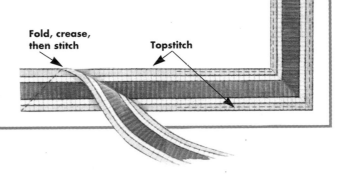

Fold, crease, then stitch

Topstitch

SHEER ROMAN SHADE

Unlined and effortless, this adaptation softly diffuses light when privacy is not an issue.

MATERIALS

* See Hardware and Notions Checklist, page 25.
* Transparent loop shade tape, ⅜-inch brass rings (or clear plastic rings for sheer fabrics)

YARDAGE AND CUTTING

1. The cut width of the shade fabric is equal to the finished width of the shade plus 4 inches for 1-inch double side hems.

2. The cut length is the finished length plus the mounting board allowance, plus 7 inches.

SEWING INSTRUCTIONS
Constructing the Shade

1. Press under and sew 1-inch double side hems.

2. Along the hem edge, press up 3 inches and stitch across the hem 1½ inches from the fold, making a rod pocket. Fold the hem up another 3 inches. Stitch across the hem ⅛ inch down from the upper folded edge.

3. Measure up from the hem edge and mark the finished length of the shade. Measure 1¾ inches (or the depth of the board) from this line toward the raw edge at the top of the shade; trim off the excess fabric. Clean-finish the raw edges with a serger or zigzag stitch.

Planning and Sewing Rings

1. On the wrong side of the shade, use a yardstick to mark the vertical lines where the rings will be sewn, keeping them even and parallel. The outermost lines should be just inside the side hems (1 inch in from outside edge). The rows in between should be spaced evenly, 8 to 12 inches apart.

2. See Simple Roman Shade, Steps 1 to 3 (pages 34 to 35), for instructions on ring positions and sewing the rings to the shade. If you are using transparent loop tape, center and sew the tape over the vertical lines, making certain that the loops on the tape align perfectly across the shade.

3. Insert the weight rod, cut ½ inch shorter than the width of the shade, through the rod pocket. If the shade is in a sheer fabric, cover the weight rod with some matching fabric (see below) before inserting it in the rod pocket. By hand, stitch closed the ends of the hem and the rod pocket.

4. Mount, rig, and dress the shade according to the instructions on pages 22 to 26.

Covering an Exposed Weight Rod

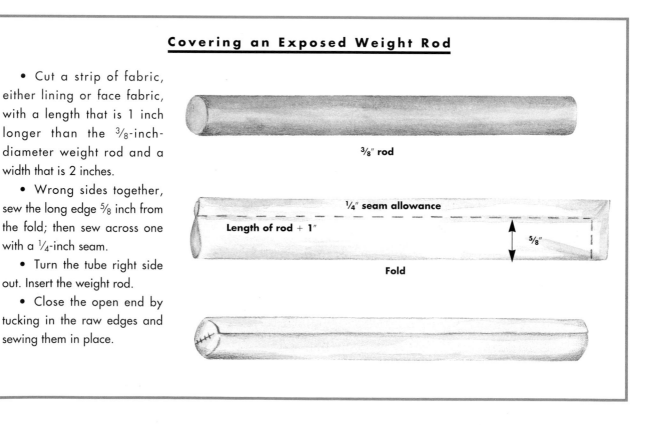

* Cut a strip of fabric, either lining or face fabric, with a length that is 1 inch longer than the ⅜-inch-diameter weight rod and a width that is 2 inches.

* Wrong sides together, sew the long edge ⅝ inch from the fold; then sew across one with a ¼-inch seam.

* Turn the tube right side out. Insert the weight rod.

* Close the open end by tucking in the raw edges and sewing them in place.

⅜″ rod

¼″ seam allowance

Length of rod + 1″

⅝″

Fold

BANDED ROMAN SHADE

*Mitering a contrast band trim defines the shade's silhouette and accents
the "tails" created by the positioning of the rigging rings. See the full treatment on page 33.*

MATERIALS

* See Hardware and Notions Checklist, page 25.
* Contrast fabric for banding and piping
* Piping cord: $\frac{5}{32}$-inch

YARDAGE AND CUTTING

1. Review the information on working with bias binding on pages 85 to 86.

2. The cut width is the same as the finished width; the cut length is the finished length plus the mounting board allowance. Cut the lining the same size as the face fabric.

3. For the 2-inch-wide banding, cut enough $3\frac{3}{4}$-inch-wide strips to bind the bottom and sides of the shade, plus a few extra inches. Cut the strip for the piping 3 inches wide by the length of the mounting board, twice the return (if needed), and 2 inches. Note: If you want the banding and piping cut on the bias, allow at least $1\frac{1}{4}$ yards of fabric so you have as few seams as possible.

SEWING INSTRUCTIONS

1. Wrong sides together, pin together the face fabric and lining.

2. Seam the banding strips to create one continuous strip of the length needed. With a $\frac{1}{2}$-inch seam, sew the banding to the sides and bottom of the shade, with the right side of the banding to the lining side of the shade. (See Binding Outward Corners, page 86.) Wrap the banding around to the front of the shade with $\frac{1}{2}$ inch of banding remaining on the lining side; miter the corners. Press under $\frac{1}{2}$ inch on the raw edge of the banding and topstitch in place.

3. Mark the finished length of the shade and clean-finish the top edge. Plan and sew ring as for Simple Roman Shade (page 34). This shade has only two vertical rows of rings, each located 5 to 8 inches in from the side edge of the shade; the distance depends on the width of the shade and how much you want the ends to fall. Keep the distance between the vertical rings to 5 to 6 inches. If the ring spacing is 5 inches, the first ring at the bottom of the shade is located $2\frac{1}{2}$ inches above the top edge of the banding, or half the space between rings.

4. Rig, mount, and dress the shade following the instructions beginning on page 22, with these additions:

• Add an extra screw eye $\frac{1}{2}$ inch in from the right end of the board so the cords will come out to the edge of the shade.

• Cut the weight rod 3 inches longer than the distance between the vertical rows of rings. Cover the rod with a tube of lining fabric. Tack the rod to the lining side of the shade just below the bottom-most rings on each side with $1\frac{1}{2}$ inches of the rod extending beyond the rings (below).

• Make piping, clean-finishing the raw edges, and staple it to the front edge of the board so that the piping lies just over the front and return edges of the board; the raw edges face the back of the board.

• Make board end covers in the banding fabric following the directions on page 82.

Half the allowance between rings

STATIONARY ROMAN SHADE

This softly draped shade eliminates cords and rings for installation where you
will not change the shade's position; it is ideal for shielding glare at the top of a window.

MATERIALS

* See Hardware and Notions Checklist, page 25, but this shade will not need the rigging hardware.

YARDAGE AND CUTTING

1. The cut width of the shade is the finished width plus 2½ inches for side hems.

2. The cut length is the desired finished length plus the mounting board allowance, 1¼ inches for the top hem, 4½ inches for the bottom hem allowance, and 7 inches for each pleat.

3. Add ¼ yard for covering the weight rod.

SEWING INSTRUCTIONS

1. Make ⅝-inch double side and top hems. Turn up bottom edge 4½ inches; turn under ½ inch on the raw edge. Stitch bottom hem in place.

2. Lay the shade out flat, wrong side up. Starting at the hem fold line (see below), measure up 7 inches and mark

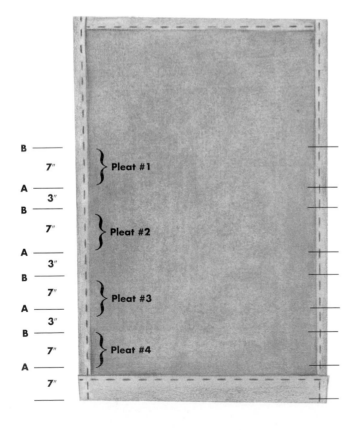

with a pin (A). Mark with a pin up another 7 inches for the first pleat (B).

3. Measure up 3 inches from B for a space and mark with a pin for the second pleat (A), followed by 7 inches for the second pleat (B). Repeat this step up the fabric for each additional pleat needed.

4. To create the pleats, start above the hemline and bring A marks up to B marks; pin in place.

5. Plan the spacing of the swoops. The pleats will be tacked in place at each side edge. Divide the space in between into equal sections as desired; the ones in the photograph are 20 inches apart. Tack each pleat in place by hand at designated divisions.

6. Cut the weight rod to ½ inch less than the width of the shade and cover it loosely with matching fabric. Along the uppermost pleat, tack the rod to the shade at each end and also at each tacked spot.

7. Mount the shade at the window using instructions under Mounting (pages 25 to 26).

TIED-UP ROMAN SHADE

Designed as a valance, not as a working shade, this Roman shade replaces rings, cords, and rigging with a long decorative ribbon.

MATERIALS

* Special mounting board (see below)
* Ribbon or decorative cord
* Self-adhesive hook-and-loop fastener

YARDAGE AND CUTTING

1. The cut width of the shade face fabric is the finished width of the shade plus 2 inches for side hems.

2. The cut length is the desired finished length plus 30 inches for the pleated-up bottom and 4½ inches for hem and board allowances. If you want more than five pleats at the bottom, add 6 inches for each additional pleat.

3. Cut lining the same length as the face fabric and the finished width of the shade.

4. Add extra yardage for covering the special mounting board (see below):

* To make the mounting board, purchase a 1 × 4-inch board the width of the shade plus twice the desired length down to the beginning of the pleats. Cut board into three pieces, one the width of the shade and two the finished length for the board "legs." Cover each piece separately with face fabric following instructions for mounting boards on page 82.

* Fasten the legs to the mounting board with nails or screws from the top of the mounting board or with angle irons on the inside.

* Adhere the hook side of the fastener tape to the narrow front edge of the legs.

SEWING INSTRUCTIONS

1. Right sides together, match and sew lining and face fabric along the side edges with a ½-inch seam. Lay lining-side up on a work surface and center the lining on the face fabric; ½ inch of face fabric will extend around to the lining side of the shade. Pin and sew the bottom edges of face and lining together. Turn shade right side out and press.

2. Clean-finish the top edge of the shade.

3. Adhere the loop side of the fastener tape, cut to the length of the mounting board leg, to the side edges of the shade, starting 3½ inches down from the top edge.

4. Fan-fold the 30 inches of fabric below the fastener tape into five pleats, making sure that the hem edge faces the window. Tack them together on the lining side at the point where you want to locate the ribbon ties. The size of the window and the desired depth of the butterflied ends will determine that placement.

5. Tie the ribbon around the board and shade at the desired points. Allow the ribbon to dangle, finishing the ends with knots, tapered ends, or a decorative cord drop.

6. Attach the shade to the mounting board, aligning the top edge of the shade with the back edge of the board.

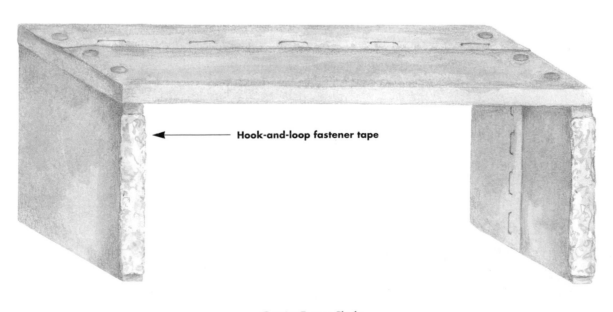

Hook-and-loop fastener tape

GROMMET AND CORD ROMAN SHADE

By placing the decorative cords and grommets on the face of the shade, they not only serve their functional duties, but also add subtle decorative detail.

MATERIALS

* See Hardware and Notions Checklist, page 25.
* Grommets: Number 1 ($^{15}/_{16}$-inch ID), 2 per pleat
* Piping cord (optional): $^5/_{32}$-inch, width of shade plus 2 inches (and two times the return if outside mounted)
* Decorative cord: $^3/_{16}$-inch to $^1/_4$-inch diameter (three times shade length plus two times shade width)
* Additional $^1/_2$ yard of fabric for covering the mounting board, weight rod, and piping cord

YARDAGE AND CUTTING

1. Plan the shade cut length and pleat spacing using the illustration on page 43 and the following notes for guidance.

• The cut length is the finished length plus 1 inch for the bottom hem, 2 inches for each pleat, and needed mounting board allowance.

• Plan pleat spacing. For standard-length windows (50 to 60 inches), plan 5 to 7 inches of space between pleats and a 3- to 4-inch allowance for a bottom flap; plan up to 11 inches of space and a 6-inch flap on long windows (90 inches).

From the *finished* shade length, subtract the amount desired for the flap to determine the pleat area (A).

Divide the result (A) by the desired spacing between pleats, rounding off fractions to the nearest whole number (B).

Adjust the spacing between the pleats by dividing the amount A by the whole number B.

• For each space, add 2 inches of fabric for a pleat.

2. The cut width is the finished width plus 2 inches for side hems.

3. Add extra fabric to cover the mounting board with self fabric and make piping cord to trim the top edge of the shade.

SEWING INSTRUCTIONS
Constructing the Shade

1. Cut fabric to the length planned. Make $^1/_2$-inch double hems on sides and bottom of the piece.

2. Pin pleats as planned, starting from the bottom of the shade. The first fold is made 1 inch above the flap allowance. The location of the next fold will be the spacing allowance plus 2 inches. Repeat this step until all pleats are formed. From the last fold, measure up spacing allowance plus 1 inch and mark for top of shade. Measure the mounting board depth beyond the top line, mark, and then cut off excess fabric, serging or zigzagging the raw edge.

3. Plan grommet placement at each fold. Follow the package directions and insert grommets through both fabric layers in each pleat, with the centers of the grommets 5 inches (or desired distance) in from the side edge. The center of each grommet should be $^3/_4$ inch in from the folded edge. At the top end of the shade, plan one more grommet halfway between the last grommet in a pleat and the top edge of the shade, but insert it through only a single layer of fabric.

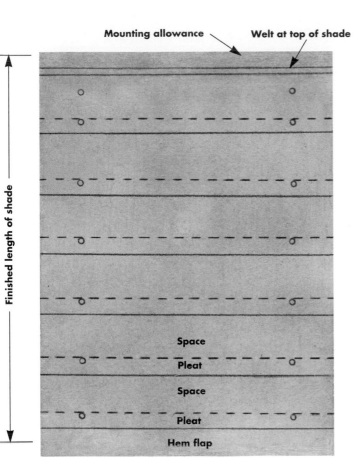

Finished length of shade (vertical label, left side)

Mounting allowance — Welt at top of shade

Space
Pleat
Space
Pleat
Hem flap

3. Staple the shade to the mounting board and then rig it. Start by making a knot in one end of the decorative cord; tie a second knot over the first. Trim cord end close to knot and cover with a dab of clear-drying glue to avoid unraveling. Bring cord over the cut end to make a neat, finished end, and tack in place to cover cut. Thread the cord up through the grommets, starting on the left bottom side of the shade. At the top grommet, thread the cord to the back of the shade, through the screw eyes toward the right. Thread the cord back to the front of the shade through the top grommet on the right side and down through the grommets to the bottom of the shade. Tie a knot in the end of the cord after it has passed through the last grommet in the same fashion as before, leaving excess cord above the knot to become the pull-up cord (below).

4. Mount the shade at the window. Pull excess cord out to the right of the right screw eye so that it falls down the side of the shade and the cords through the shade grommets are taut. Tie the excess cord into a knot near the screw eye and twist the hanging cords together.

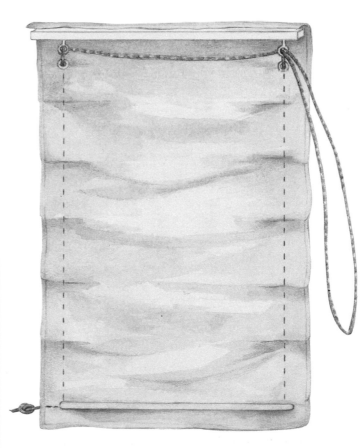

Mounting and Rigging the Shade

1. Optional piping trim on board edge:

• Cover piping cord, cut to mounting board width, with self fabric and turn in ½ inch of fabric at the ends.

• On the shade, trim off mounting board allowance less ½ inch. Cut a fabric strip for new mounting board allowance, twice the allowance width by the length of the board and ½-inch seam allowance all around. Fold in half lengthwise, turn in ½ inch on each end. Baste raw edges together.

• Baste the piping to the top edge of the shade. Sew the new board allowance strip over the piping, matching raw edges. Clean-finish the raw edges.

• Staple the shade to the mounting board so piping sits at the front edge. If the shade is outside-mounted, the piping cord should be along the returns also; cover the rigging with board end covers (see page 82).

2. Cut weight rod to 3 inches longer than the horizontal distance between the grommets and cover it with a tube of self fabric. Horizontally center the covered rod on the back of the shade and tack it there at the top of the two lowest grommets.

DECORATIVE SHAPED HEM FOR ROMAN SHADES

By varying the shape of the hem edge of a Roman shade or adding a decorative trim to it, you can give a dashing look to an otherwise conventional treatment.

You will need to add inches to the cut length of your shade to make the shape or trim visible once the shade is raised. On a plain, unadorned shade the standard finished hem depth is half the distance between the rows of rings. If you want 3 inches of decorative hem to show, a common depth, add 3 inches to the plain hem depth. However, the hem can be more or less than that—let the proportions of your shade be your guide.

Preconstruction Considerations for Lined and Unlined Shades

The shade instructions for both lined and unlined Roman shades are based on a 6-inch hem, of which 3 inches will show when the shade is in the raised position, and ring spacing of 6 inches. For shallower or deeper folds, adjust the ring spacing from 5 to 8 inches. Keep in mind that the first pleat of the shade covers half the distance between the rings, so adjustments to the hem depth and cut length measurements will probably be necessary.

If you are planning to add only a top-applied style trim to a straight hem, but need more hem space at the bottom of the shade, follow the Simple Roman Shade instructions (page 34), increasing the 3-inch hem folds in Step 1 of Constructing the Shade to 6 inches, or desired depth. The trim is applied to the decorative hem area before proceeding to Step 2.

If you are planning a shaped hem, make a pattern for the shape on a 6-inch-wide piece of paper, cut to the width of the shade. Mark off 1 inch at each side edge for the hem allowance and draw the desired shape in between. If your fabric has a pattern that inherently lends itself to shaping, plan the bottom fold or seam line accordingly, allowing for $\frac{1}{2}$-inch seam allowance there. Sometimes this situation means that the two-layer facing needs to be cut separately. In the side hem allowance, mark a stitch line 3 inches up from the bottom edge and adjust the hem shaping at the sides to meet this line. Cut out the bottom shape.

If you want to give your hem some additional body, cut a piece of buckram or fleece batting whose length is the finished width of the shade and whose width is $\frac{3}{8}$ inch less than the depth of the hem. Insert this piece in hem area.

Lined Shaped-Hem Roman Shade

The design of the fabric itself may suggest an interesting hem shaping.

MATERIALS
* Review instructions for Simple Roman Shade, page 34.

YARDAGE AND CUTTING

1. The cut width of the shade face fabric is the finished width of the shade plus 2 inches for side hems. The lining is cut without the 2-inch side hem allowance.

2. The cut length of the face fabric starts with the finished length plus mounting board allowance plus 7 inches. For the decorative hem, add three times the desired depth of the *decorative* hem portion plus 1½ inches for seam allowance. For example, if 3 inches of hem is to show, add 10½ inches for the decorative hem to the starting cut length.

3. Cut the lining fabric the finished length plus the board allowance plus 13 inches.

SEWING INSTRUCTIONS
Constructing the Shade

1. On the hem edge of the face fabric, press 6½ inches to the wrong side. Turn that 6½-inch folded section, now a two-layer facing piece, back on itself to the right side of the fabric. There will be three layers of fabric with a fold and raw edge at the bottom of the piece.

2. Follow the instructions in the Preconstruction Considerations for Lined and Unlined Shades (page 44) to make the hem pattern. Lay that pattern over the hem allowance on the wrong side and ½ inch up from the bottom edge. Trace the pattern onto the fabric and sew along this line. Trim the seam allowance to ¼ inch, clipping as needed; turn and press. See the below-right illustration.

3. On the lining fabric, press up 6 inches and stitch across the hem 1½ inches from the hem fold, making a rod pocket. Fold the lining up another 6 inches and press and pin to make a 6-inch double hem.

4. With right sides together, place the lining so that the bottom of its hem is ¼ inch above the highest point on the decorative hem of the face fabric, thus preventing the lining from being visible from the right side of the shade. Match the side edges, pin, and sew together with ½-inch seams.

5. Lay out the shade with the lining side up. Make a small slit, ¾ inch wide, at one end of the rod pocket, cutting through the top layer of lining only. The rod will be inserted here later.

6. Turn the shade right side out, center the lining on the face fabric, and press. The lining is narrower than the face fabric, so ½ inch of face fabric will extend to the lining side of the shade.

7. From the lining side, stitch the bottom hems in place 5¾ inches up from the bottom edge of the face fabric.

8. On the lining side of the shade, measure up from the hem edge and mark the finished length of the shade. Measure 1¾ inches (or the depth of the board) from this line toward the raw edge at the top of the shade; trim off the excess fabric and lining. Clean-finish the raw edges with a serger or zigzag stitch.

Planning and Sewing Rings

1. On the lining side of the shade, use a yardstick to mark the vertical lines for the rings, keeping the rows even and parallel. At the outside edges, the lines should be 1 inch in from the edge. The rows in between should be spaced evenly, 8 to 12 inches apart. It is very important for rings,

cords, and screw eyes to be perfectly aligned. See illustrations under Simple Roman Shade, page 34.

2. Mark the ring positions along the vertical lines, the spacing having been decided in the Preconstruction Considerations on page 44. Position the first ring at the bottom of the shade at the top of the rod pocket; the last ring at the top must be 3 inches or more down from the top finished line of the shade. All the rings must align perfectly across the shade.

3. Sew the rings to the shade at the marked spots, by hand or machine zigzag stitch, using thread that matches the face fabric. Be sure to catch a tiny amount of the face fabric as you sew. (To sew rings on by machine, use a zigzag stitch and lower the feed dogs; cover rings with 8 to 10 stitches. You can move from one ring spot to the next without cutting threads.)

4. Turn out the bottom hem to expose the rod pocket made on the lining. Cut a weight rod 1¼ inches shorter than the finished width of the shade and insert it through the slit you made in constructing the shade. Stitch the slit closed and turn the hem down again.

5. Mount, rig, and dress the shade according to the instructions on pages 22 to 26.

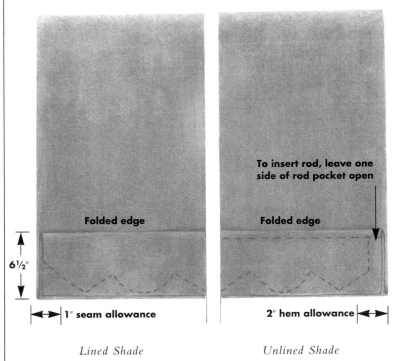

Lined Shade *Unlined Shade*

UNLINED SHAPED-HEM ROMAN SHADE

Roman shades are suitable for outdoor use as well as for interior windows.

MATERIALS

* Review instructions for Simple Roman Shade, page 34.

YARDAGE AND CUTTING

1. The shade cut width is the finished width of the shade plus 4 inches for 1-inch double side hems.

2. The cut length starts with the finished length plus mounting board allowance plus 7 inches. For the decorative hem, add three times the desired depth of the *decorative* hem portion plus 1½ inches for seam allowance. For example, if 3 inches of hem is to show, add 10½ inches for the decorative hem to the starting cut length.

SEWING INSTRUCTIONS
Constructing the Shade

1. On the hem edge of the fabric, press 6½ inches to the wrong side. Stitch across the hem 1½ inches from the fold, making a rod pocket.

2. Turn that 6½-inch folded section, now a two-layer facing piece, back on itself to the right side of the fabric. There will be three layers of fabric with a fold and raw edge at the bottom of the piece.

3. Follow the instructions in the Preconstruction Considerations (page 44) to make the hem pattern so that it covers only the finished width of the shade, not the cut width.

4. Lay that pattern over the hem allowance on the wrong side and ½ inch up from the bottom edge. Trace the pattern onto the fabric, including the side seams that are 2 inches in from the cut edge. Sew along the shaped line and up the sides of the hem. On one side edge, sew all the way up to the top folded edge of the hem. On the other side, stitch up the side only to the rod pocket stitch line. See the illustration on page 45.

5. Trim the seam allowance to ¼ inch on the shaped edge and on the two top layers of the side hem allowance (the facing); leave the bottom layer on the sides untrimmed.

Clip curves and points as needed; turn and press. Pin the top folded hem edge in place.

6. Press under 1-inch double side hems, carrying these hems down into the bottom hem area. Stitch them in place above the bottom hem area.

7. Stitch across the hem ¼ inch down from the top fold, leaving 2 inches unstitched at the end where the rod pocket is open. If you do not want the stitching to show on the right side of the shade, hand sew the folded edge in place.

8. On the wrong side of the shade, measure up from the hem edge and mark the finished length of the shade. Measure 1¾ inches (or the depth of the mounting board) from this line toward the raw edge at the top of the shade; trim off the excess fabric. Clean-finish the raw edges with a serger or zigzag stitch.

Planning and Sewing Rings

1. On the lining side of the shade, use a yardstick to mark the vertical lines for the rings, keeping the rows even and parallel. At the outside edges, the lines should be 1 inch in from the edge, just inside the side hems. The rows in between should be spaced evenly, 8 to 12 inches apart. It is very important for rings, cords, and screw eyes to be perfectly aligned. See illustrations under Simple Roman Shade, page 34.

2. Mark the ring positions along the vertical lines, the spacing having been decided in the Preconstruction Considerations for Lined and Unlined Shades on page 44. Position the first ring at the bottom of the shade at the top of the rod pocket; the last ring at the top must be 3 inches or more down from the top finished line of the shade. All the rings must align perfectly across the shade.

3. Sew the rings to the shade at the marked spots, by hand or machine zigzag stitch, using thread that matches the fabric. (To sew rings on by machine, use a zigzag stitch and lower the feed dogs; cover rings with 8 to 10 stitches. You can move from one ring spot to the next without cutting threads.)

4. Cut the weight rod to ½ inch less than the finished shade width and insert it in the rod pocket. Finish the stitching across the fold and close that end of the rod pocket.

5. Mount, rig, and dress the shade according to the instructions on pages 22 to 26.

HOBBLED ROMAN SHADE

Although the "hobbled" construction requires twice the fabric of a flat, more tailored Roman shade, the folds soften the window even when the shade is lowered. It's a wonderful idea for adding interest to a solid-fabric shade.

MATERIALS

* See Hardware and Notions Checklist, page 25.
* Twill tape: 1/2-inch
* Narrow wood lattice slats or wood dowels—one for each pleat
* Cornice

YARDAGE AND CUTTING

1. Decide the desired finished length of the shade; divide this length by six to determine the number of pleats needed. Round off fractions to the nearest whole number. The cut length is then the finished length, 12 inches of fabric for each pleat, and 6 inches for the bottom hem plus the board mounting allowance.

2. The cut width is the finished width plus 2 inches. The lining is cut the finished width of the shade.

SEWING INSTRUCTIONS
Constructing the Shade

1. Right sides together, sew the decorator fabric and lining along the side edges with a 1/2-inch seam. Press seams open and turn piece right side out. One half inch of the decorator fabric will turn to the wrong side of the shade.

2. Press up 3 inches at the bottom of the shade. Stitch across the shade 1 1/4 inches from the folded edge to create a pocket for the weight bar. Fold up hem another 3 inches for a double hem. Sew hem in place by hand or machine at upper fold line.

Marking the Pleats

1. Lay out the shade, lining side up, to mark the pleat lines. The first line is the hem stitching line; the second is 12 inches up from that one. Draw a faint line across the shade at that location. Continue to mark lines 12 inches apart all

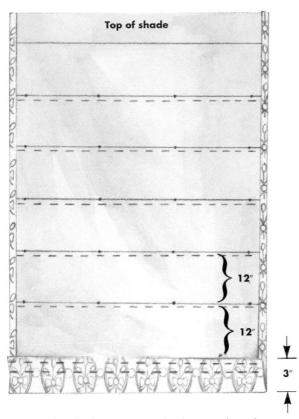

Top of shade

} 12"

} 12"

3"

the way up the shade. Counting the hem stitching line you should have one more line than number of planned pleats; the last drawn line is the top of the shade. Pin across all lines (above).

2. Sew across each marked line from edge to edge. Sew across the shade again below each line to create a pocket for the slats, except for the topmost line. The pocket must be large enough to accommodate the slats or dowels.

3. From the topmost line, measure up the depth of the mounting board and cut off excess fabric. Clean-finish the raw edge.

4. Plan and mark on each of the horizontally stitched lines (the ones drawn in Step 1) the vertical spacing of the rings. The first row should be $1\frac{1}{4}$ inches in from each side edge. Additional rows in between should be spaced equally 8 to 12 inches apart. Press the shade.

Creating the Pleats

1. Cut one piece of twill tape for each vertical row, each the finished length of the shade. Lay the tapes out on a table, side by side, taping the ends to the table to hold them in place. Make the first ring mark across the row of tapes 1 inch in from a cut end. Mark ring placement down the tapes with 6-inch spacing, having one more mark than the number of planned pleats.

2. Pin the twill tapes to the lining side of the shade, matching the ring marks on the shade with the ring marks on the tape. At the bottom hem, open up the hem stitching enough to tuck in the end of the tape; re-sew. At the top edge, allow 1 inch of tape beyond the topmost mark. Sew across twill tape at each ring mark. Then sew a ring to each of these spots by hand or with a zigzag stitch on a machine, reinforcing the bottom row of rings as they carry the weight of the shade (below).

3. At one end of each pocket sewn in Marking the Pleats, Step 2, break a few stitches in the pocket area along the edge. Insert the slats, cut 1 inch shorter than the shade width, into these pockets. Into the pocket sewn into the bottom hem, insert the weight rod cut to the same length as the slats. Hand stitch the ends closed. (If wood dowels are not long enough, splice them by gluing two pieces to a split length of a sturdy soda straw.)

Mounting and Rigging the Shade

1. Follow the instructions in Mounting and Rigging on pages 22 to 26, or construct an upholstered cornice (page 80).

2. If using a cornice, attach the shade to the back of the face board with staples or hook-and-loop fastener tape. Position the screw eyes in the bottom of the top board above each row of rings. Then rig and mount at the window as in the step above.

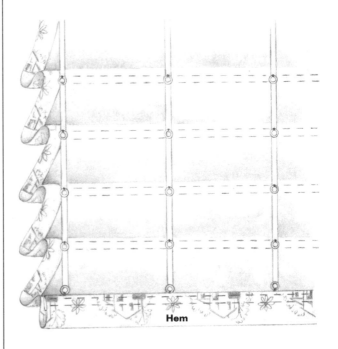

Hem

Creating Balloon and Austrian Shades
Basics, Patterns, and Instructions

Balloon and Austrian shades are both closely related to the Roman shade and share many instructions for construction, mounting, and rigging. However, both the balloon and Austrian shade (and their many variations) generally differ in this important detail: They have extra fullness, both horizontally and vertically. This gives them a softer appeal than most Roman shades and also involves a little more calculation and fabric manipulation along the road to their creation.

The eye-catching balloon shade is a soft shade closely related to the Roman shade in construction, but using more fabric so that in the raised position, it billows into soft poufs along the bottom edge. Balloon shades come in three basic styles: cloud, shirred, and pleated. A cloud shade, a casual cousin of the shirred balloon shade, has just enough fullness in the horizontal shirring to soften the tailored look of the flat Roman. The shirred balloon has quite a bit of fullness in the heading, often created with decorative shirring tapes. The pleated balloon features inverted box pleats across the heading. When pulled up, this shade exposes the horizontal fullness "hidden" in the pleats. The shade may be flat when lowered or may be created with extra length to feature soft poufs at the lower edge, even when the shade is in its lowered position.

A melding of tailored and soft elements, the balloon shade lends itself to a wide variety of situations. It's the perfect choice when a Roman shade is too understated and an Austrian shade is too ornate; it softens rooms with too many angles and adds refinement to rooms in need of definition.

All three styles of balloon shades draw up in the same manner as Roman shades and can be constructed to release to full window length or be made shorter for permanently securing at valance length. Like Roman shades, balloon shades can be lined to give them a richer appearance.

The Austrian shade is an elegant style that lends itself to formal dining and living rooms, as well as bedrooms and baths. A variation on the Roman shade, it features vertical shirring distributed along its entire length, which transforms the tailored folds of the Roman style into soft, draping scallops. The shade is gathered vertically to the desired finished length, then pulled up with the same rigging used for the basic Roman shade.

Balloon and Austrian Shade Basics

- **FABRICS.** The allure of balloon and Austrian shades is in their softness and fullness. Therefore, softer-handed, lighter-weight fabrics are recommended. For help in choosing fabrics to suit your personal taste, decor, and preferred care methods, refer to Choosing Fabric, page 17, and the Fiber Wear and Care chart on page 20.
- **LINING.** Although balloon shades may be lined, Austrians rarely are lined, and interlining—which adds bulk—is not appropriate for either.
- **MEASURING.** Always measure each window carefully, double-checking each measurement to avoid accidentally sabotaging your project before you begin. Refer to Measuring and Estimating, page 27, for specific guidelines.
- **ESTIMATING YARDAGE.** As noted earlier, every

PRECEDING PAGES: *Detailing the top of a balloon shade is easy with readily available tapes that are straight stitched to the fabric and then shirred with cords to create interesting patterns—from simple pencil pleats to the illusion of diamond smocking. Complete instructions for this shade are on page 54.* OPPOSITE: *If your balloon shade will never be lowered, you can save fabric and labor by creating a balloon valance.*

window treatment has its own subtleties and special allowances. In most cases, however, the Basic Yardage Formula on page 28 will provide a framework for beginning. The allowances noted in Pleated Balloon Shade on page 74 and Sheer Austrian Shade on page 72 may help, but to determine allowances for shade variations, refer to the instructions with each project.

- **WEIGHT BAR.** Like their Roman relative, both balloon and Austrian shades are constructed with weight bars near their lower edge to help them operate smoothly. Some shades have rod pockets built into their hem area for the bar (refer to Roman Shade Basics, page 32, for details), while others hold the rod in place by tacking it just below the bottom row of rings, or sometimes by way of loops made at the end of the shade tapes. In the latter two cases, the bar is covered in a fabric casing to allow it to be tacked to the ring area or to the loops.
- **POUFED HEMS.** If you don't want your balloon shade to be completely flat when let down, add fabric for one or more permanent "poufs" at the lower edge. This will require an additional 18 to 40 inches of fabric, depending on your windows. For details, refer to page 54.

Stitch the tape lengths in place and pull up the cords to create the desired shade finished length. *Do not* cut the cords! When it's time to clean your shade, you'll need to untie them to flatten the shade. For complete instructions on determining the tape placement and applying the tape, refer to Sheer Austrian Shade on page 72.

• **HARDWARE AND MOUNTING.** Both balloon and Austrian shades may be inside- or outside-mounted. For details on all of the hardware and notions required, plus mounting tips and tricks, refer to pages 22 to 26. Also refer to the specific instructions for the treatments featured here in Part 3.

• **DRESSING AND STUFFING.** Pull the shade up and loop the cord on the cleat to hold the shade in the "up" position while you work. At each row of rings, pull and shape the folds so that they lie smoothly one on top of the other. Evenly distribute the fullness in the balloon sections by fanfolding the fabric with your fingers. If your fabric needs "assistance" to maintain the billowing effect in the poufs, fill each pouf with scrunched-up nylon net or dry cleaner plastic bags. If you plan to raise and lower the shade on a regular basis, just fill the permanent poufs at the bottom.

• **SHIRRING AUSTRIAN SHADES.** Austrian shades owe their reputation for opulence to ample vertical fullness—usually three times the finished length. This fullness is shirred up to the desired length (to the sill or the floor are common choices) through the use of Austrian shade tape, a purchased tape featuring two shirring cords and either rings or cross threads for stringing the shade with cords. The result is a series of 9- to 12-inch-wide scallops undulating across the width of the shade and all the way down its length.

To make an Austrian shade, you'll need one more shirring tape length than you have scallops (in general, an uneven number of scallops looks best).

• **CARE AND UPKEEP.** "Dust" and launder balloon and Austrian shades as described for Roman shades in Roman Shade Basics on page 32. However, a word of caution: Caring for an Austrian shade can be expensive if dry cleaning is required. Choosing a lightweight, drapable fabric that can be washed and dried will help defray this cost, but will require some extra planning and effort on your part. As noted for Roman shades, some dressing and training will likely be required until poufs and scallops develop "memory."

BALLOON SHADE WITH SHIRR TAPE TOP

Balloon shades are usually planned and constructed with an uneven number of scallops, but over French doors, two scallops is more effective.

MATERIALS

* See Hardware and Notions Checklist, page 25.
* Four-cord shirr tape, the width of the ungathered shade (regular tape or one with woven-in loop fastener)
* Purchased wide double-fold bias tape or custom-made binding from contrast fabric
* *With regular shirr tape:* fabric mounting strip—a piece of fabric the length of the mounting board plus twice the return plus 1 inch and a width of 4 inches
* *With woven-in loop fastener shirr tape:* hook fastener tape the same length as fabric mounting strip

YARDAGE AND CUTTING

1. The cut width of the shade is 1¾ to 2 times the width and returns of the mounting board. Because the sides and bottom are bound with bias trim, there are no hem allowances. To be sure that pattern motifs, stripes, and seams fall in appropriate places, plan your shade on paper.

• Plan the outermost vertical rows of rings based on the outside edges of the glass area of your window—or other appropriate spot—and mark the mounting board accordingly. The "butterfly tails" will be created by the fabric to the left and right of those outside rows. The rows in between those points should be equally spaced, no more than 27 inches apart. Screw eyes will be placed on the mounting board to correspond to the rows of rings.

• To determine the amount of fabric in each tail section, multiply the inches from the last screw eye to the end of the board (for inside mount) and around the return by the fullness factor. For the scallop sections, multiply the inches in each space between screw eyes by the fullness factor.

2. The cut length for a full-length shade is the window height (or desired mounting height) plus 17 inches for three permanent poufs and hem and top allowances. For a shade that will be stationary, cut the desired finished length plus 27 inches for five permanent poufs and allowances.

3. The lining is cut the same size as the face fabric.

4. If using custom-made binding, cut from the coordinating fabric enough 2½-inch-wide bias strips to go across the bottom and up both sides of the shade.

SEWING INSTRUCTIONS
Constructing the Shade

1. Seam face fabric and lining widths as planned. Wrong sides together, pin face and lining. Bind the side and bottom edges with a contrast binding, ½ inch wide, following the instructions for Working with Bias Binding, page 85.

2. Press under 2 inches at top edge of shade to the lining side; trim away lining to fold line. Sew the shirring tape across the top, starting the tape ½ inch down from the top folded edge. Turn under ½ inch on each end of tape and pull out the cords. Stitch at the top and bottom of the tape and on each side of all cords.

3. Plan and sew the rings to the back of the shade as planned above and following the instructions under Planning and Sewing Rings in Simple Roman Shade, page 34. Note that the first ring at the bottom of this shade is attached 12 inches up from the bottom bound edge, and other rings are spaced 5 to 6 inches apart, depending on how deep you want the folds.

4. Mark with pins on the shirr tape the location of the rows of rings. On a small shade, secure the cords at one end with a knot or by stitching over them well; on a large shade secure the cords in the center of the tape. Gather the fabric by pulling the cords at the end(s) until the shade is the width of the mounting board (and returns). Adjust the gathers evenly.

Installing the Shade

1. Attach the shade to a mounting board and rig it according the instructions on pages 22 to 26, with these additions:

• To create permanent poufs at the bottom of the shade, tie the first three to five rings together and then thread cord up through the rest of the rings.

• If you are planning a staple attachment, use a fabric mounting strip, cut as directed in Materials: Fold the strip in half lengthwise, turning in ½ inch on the short ends. Clean-finish the raw edges with a serger or zigzag stitch.

With pins, mark the strip for the return and location of rows of rings to correspond to the screw eyes on the mounting board.

Pin and sew this strip to the wrong side of the top of the valance. Align the bottom edge of the mounting strip with a "rib" on the shirr tape below the topmost cord. Sew along the topmost stitching line on the shirr tape.

Staple the valance to the mounting board so that the seam between the valance and mounting strip rests at the top front edge of the board.

• If you are using hook-and-loop fastener tape, attach the loop side to the narrow front edge and sides of the mounting board.

• The weight rod, cut to 3 inches longer than the distance between the two outer screw eyes, is handled in the same fashion as for Banded Roman Shade, page 38. Use the spacing of the screw eyes to mark the location of the vertical rows of rings on the rod cover and then tack it appropriately at the bottom row of rings.

2. Mount the shade at the window as planned. Dress it as instructed on page 53.

12" to 15"

EMBELLISHED BALLOON SHADE WITH ROSETTES

Creating your own trim details from coordinating fabrics is less expensive than working with purchased decorative trims, and it's easier to find the perfect match.

MATERIALS

* See Hardware and Notions Checklist, page 25.
* Coordinating fabric for binding, contrast lining on bottom edges, creating choux rosettes, and making pleated ruff at top of shade
* Decorative cord
* Optional: Perfect Pleater™ for making the pleated ruff. (See Resource Guide, page 94.)

YARDAGE AND CUTTING

1. When planning the mounting position for this shade, note that the 3-inch ruff sits above the mounting board.

2. Refer to the Yardage and Cutting section of Balloon Shade with Shirr Tape Top (page 54), making the following changes:

* The cut width of the shade is 1½ to 1¾ times the width and returns of the mounting board.
* The cut length "extra" for full-length shade changes to 21 inches and the stationary one to 31 inches.

3. From the coordinating fabric, cut the following in addition to the binding:

* For the contrast lining at the bottom edge, cut a strip 8½ inches wide by the cut width of the shade.
* For the choux rosettes, cut one 14-inch circle for each rosette, planning one for each row of rings.
* For the 3-inch pleated ruff, cut 7-inch-wide fabric strips (cut on the straight or bias), planning three times fullness.

SEWING INSTRUCTIONS

Constructing the Basic Shade

1. Seam face fabric, lining, and coordinating lining widths if needed. Press under ½ inch on one long edge of coordinating lining strip. Pin it to the bottom of the right side of the lining piece, aligning the raw edges. Topstitch the strip to the lining close to the folded edge.

2. Wrong sides together, pin face and lining. Bind the side and bottom edges with binding, following the instructions under Working with Bias Binding, page 85. Baste the top edges together.

3. Plan and sew the rings to the back of the shade as planned above and following the instructions under Balloon Shade with Shirr Tape Top (page 55). Note that the first ring at

the bottom of the shade is attached 8 inches up from the bottom edge where the coordinating lining meets the regular lining.

4. Gather the top edge of the shade up to the width of the mounting board and its returns.

Making the Pleated Ruff

1. Seam the coordinating strips for the ruff as needed. Press in half lengthwise and baste edges together, turning in ½ inch at each end of the strip to finish the ends.

2. Pleat up and press the strip into ½-inch pleats until the strip is the width of the gathered shade. To stabilize the strip, pin it to a piece of paper; adding-machine tape works well. Stitch the pleats in place ⅜ inch in from the raw edge.

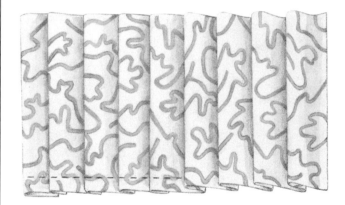

3. Right sides together, sew the pleated strip to the gathered shade. Clean-finish the seam and press it toward the shade. The seam will stay in that position if you topstitch it close to the seam line.

4. Staple the shade to the narrow front edge of the mounting board, centering the seam between the shade and the ruff on that narrow edge. Ease the shade onto the board.

5. Glue or hand tack the decorative cord over the seam line and staples.

Finishing

1. Prepare and attach the weight rod as in Balloon Shade with Shirr Tape Top, page 54.

2. Make the choux rosettes (page 58). Pin or hand sew the rosettes to the shade at each row of rings over the permanent poufs.

3. Mount and dress the shade at the window according to the instructions on pages 22 to 26.

These puffy rosettes are a delightful way to dress up a variety of window coverings, adding style, character, and old-fashioned charm. They usually are made in the window treatment fabric, but they also can be created in contrast fabric. Use them to highlight a particular feature, enhance your design's decorative appeal, or conceal stitches or joins.

1. For a 3½-inch rosette, cut a 14-inch-diameter circle from the desired fabric. Also cut a 7-inch-diameter circle from paper and fold the paper circle to divide it into eight equal pie-shaped sections. For larger rosettes, start with a larger fabric circle and a paper circle half its diameter; for paper circles larger than 9 inches in diameter, divide the circle into sixteen sections.

2. Using a hand needle and doubled heavy-duty thread, run a row of gathering stitches around the circumference of the fabric circle, ⅜ inch from the edge. Pull up the threads to gather the circle edges tautly, and tack to secure the gathers.

3. Center the gathers at the circle's center to create a smaller circle. Using an air- or water-soluble marker and the paper circle as a guide, mark the outer edge of each pie-shaped section on the ungathered side.

4. To pouf the rosette, bring the outer edge marking of each section to the circle's center and, using a hand needle and doubled heavy-duty thread, tack it in place. Arrange the poufs as desired.

5. To attach a rosette to the window treatment, use pins, hook-and-loop tape, or glue.

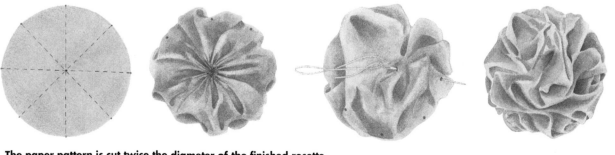

The paper pattern is cut twice the diameter of the finished rosette.

SHEER CLOUD SHADE

This soft cloud shade is simply shirred on a standard curtain rod. The "butterfly tails" are a result of the ring placement and rigging of the shade.

MATERIALS

* See Hardware and Notions Checklist, page 25.
* Curtain rod, spring-tension rod (clear rod suggested with sheer fabrics)

YARDAGE AND CUTTING

1. The cut width of the shade is at least $1\frac{1}{4}$, but no more than $1\frac{1}{2}$, times the width to be covered, plus 2 inches for side hem allowance. (Add twice the return depth to the cut width for an outside mount.)

2. The cut length of the shade is the finished length plus 15 inches (5-inch pleat spacing) for fullness at the shade bottom and $3\frac{1}{4}$ inches for rod casing and hem allowances.

If you want a header, add twice that desired depth.

SEWING INSTRUCTIONS

1. Make $\frac{1}{2}$-inch double hems on sides and bottom of shade piece.

2. To create rod casing at top edge of shade piece, press under $2\frac{1}{4}$ inches. Turn under $\frac{1}{2}$ inch on raw edge. Topstitch $\frac{1}{4}$ inch in from lower folded edge to create $1\frac{1}{2}$-inch casing. If adding a header, the first turn under will be $2\frac{1}{4}$ inches plus the header height; stitch across the shade the header height down from the folded edge before making the $\frac{1}{2}$ inch turn under.

3. This shade has only two vertical rows of rings. Plan their location based on the width of the shade and how much you want the ends to "butterfly." We suggest the rows be 6 to 8 inches in from the outside edges of the finished shade on a single window. The amount of fabric in the butterfly tails will be $1\frac{1}{4}$ to $1\frac{1}{2}$ times that measurement. For further details on planning and sewing rings, see Simple Roman Shade, page 34, and sew the first bottom ring at the top of the hem.

4. To rig the shade, tie the bottom three rings together and then pass the cord up through the rest of the rings. Allow enough extra cord at each row to go through screw eyes and down the side of the shade.

5. See Mounting and Rigging, page 22, for mounting information. The screw eyes used for rigging the shade will be 6 to 8 inches in from the ends of the mounting surface.

6. Prepare the weight rod as in Balloon Shade with Shirr Tape Top, page 54, tacking it where the three rings are tied together.

7. Shirr the shade on the rod and install it at the window. Thread the cords through the screw eyes and finish the rigging as described on page 26.

CLOUD SHADE WITH CORD

*A decorative cord with figure-eight knots and a coordinating fringe dress up
this interpretation of a cloud shade.*

MATERIALS

* See Hardware and Notions Checklist, page 25.
* Decorative cord: ½-inch diameter
* One-cord shirr tape or fine nylon cord
* Fringe trim

YARDAGE AND CUTTING

1. The cut width of the shade face fabric is 1½ times the width to be covered, plus 2 inches for side hem allowance. Don't forget to include the returns in your calculation of the finished width. The lining is cut without the 2-inch hem allowance.

2. The cut length of the shade face and lining fabrics is the finished length plus 15½ inches for fullness and seam at the shade bottom and 3¼ inches for top turn-down allowance.

SEWING INSTRUCTIONS

1. Baste fringe to the bottom of face fabric piece, stopping the fringe 2 inches in from each side.

2. With right sides together, pin and sew face and lining with ½-inch seams, matching side raw edges.

3. Lining side up, adjust the fabrics so that the lining sits centered on the face fabric and seams are pressed inward. Pin and sew the bottom seam. Turn shade right side out and press.

4. At top edge of shade, press down 3¼ inches. If fabric is heavy, trim away lining above the fold line. Clean-finish the raw edge.

5. To create the shirred top, draw a line 2 inches down from the folded edge. Sew shirr tape or zigzag over nylon cord, centered over this line.

6. This shade has only two vertical rows of rings. Plan their location based on the glass area of your window and mark the mounting board accordingly. Attach screw eyes at these points. Measure the front of the board from one of those points to the end and along the return; multiply that number by 1½, the shade fullness factor. On the shade, the rows of rings will be located that distance in from the side edges. For further details on planning and sewing rings, see Simple Roman Shade, page 34.

7. To rig the shade, tie the bottom three rings together and then pass the cord up through the rest of the rings. Allow enough extra cord at each row to go through screw eyes and down the side of the shade.

8. Prepare and attach the weight rod as in Balloon Shade with Shirr Tape Top, page 54.

9. Pull the cord on the shirr tape to gather the top of the shade to the mounting board length, including returns. Staple the shade to the narrow front edge of the board, centering the cord on that edge. Glue or hand tack the decorative cord over the shirred cord and staples, making a figure-eight knot at the two rows of rings (below).

10. Finish the rigging by threading the cords through the screw eyes. Install the shade at the window and complete the installation as described in Mounting and Rigging on pages 22 to 26.

Creating the Perfect Knot

Knotted cord is a beautiful way to acent shades. A figure-eight knot highlighting each pleat or accentuating a heading makes elegant detailing. Arrange the cord following the illustration before pulling the knot taut.

RUFFLED BALLOON SHADE ON MOUNTING BOARD

*On a wide span of windows, dividing the width into smaller shades is often advisable.
Here, a ruffle cut from the dominant stripe in the shade fabric edges each shade and integrates the
individual shades beautifully.*

MATERIALS

* See Hardware and Notions Checklist, page 25.
* Extra fabric for ruffles
* Two-cord shirr tape, the width of the ungathered shade
* Fabric mounting strip: a piece of fabric the length of the mounting board plus twice the return plus 1 inch and a width of 4 inches

YARDAGE AND CUTTING

1. See the Yardage and Cutting information in Balloon Shade with Shirr Tape Top, page 54, for the base shade. Plan two times fullness.

2. When planning the mounting position for this shade, note that a ruff sits above the mounting board about 1½ inches.

3. Plan for the ruffle trim by referring to Creating Ruffles, page 65. Cut the ruffle strips 4½ inches wide for a 3½-inch finished ruffle; or the desired finished width plus 1 inch for hems.

• The ruffles, gathered to 1½ times fullness, are on the side and bottom edges. Allow an extra 12 inches so you can put extra fullness in the corners of the shade.

• Consider editing your fabric to use it creatively for the ruffle. For example, the dominant stripe in the fabric was used for this photographed shade.

• After you determine the length of ruffle strip needed for your shade and decide whether you want to cut on the straight or bias of the fabric, plan the cutting layout on paper to determine the additional yardage needed.

SEWING INSTRUCTIONS

Constructing the Shade

1. Seam face fabric and lining widths as planned. Right sides together and edges even, sew face and lining along side and bottom edges only. Turn right side out; press.

2. Press under 2 inches at the top edge of the shade to the lining side; trim away lining to fold line. Pin top allowance in place.

3. Cut and seam the strips for the ruffle and then follow the instructions for creating topstitched ruffles. The gather/

stitching line should be ½ inch down from one edge.

4. Sew the ruffles around the sides and bottom of the shade front, pushing extra ruffles into the corners. Place the stitching line of the ruffle ¼ inch in from the edges.

5. Sew shirr tape across the top of the shade, starting the tape 1¼ inches down from the top folded edge, so that the stitching line will be 1½ inches down from that edge. Turn under ½ inch on each end of the tape and release the cord ends. Stitch at the top and bottom of the tape and through the middle.

6. Mark and sew the rings to the back of the shade as planned under the Yardage and Cutting section at left, and then follow the instructions under Planning and Sewing Rings in Simple Roman Shade, page 34. At the outside edges, the vertical rows will be ½ inch in from the ruffle stitching line. The first ring at the bottom will be ½ inch above the ruffle stitching line.

Finishing the Shade

1. Mark with pins on the shirr tape the location of the rows of rings. On a small shade, secure the cords at one end with a knot or by stitching over them well; on a large shade secure the cord in the center of the tape. Gather the shade by pulling the cords at the end(s) until the shade is the width of the mounting board (and returns). Adjust the gathers evenly.

2. Attach the shade to a mounting board using a fabric mounting strip as instructed under Balloon Shade with Shirr Tape Top. Align the bottom edge of the mounting strip with the center stitch line on the shirr tape.

3. Cut the weight rod to 1 inch longer than the distance between the two outer screw eyes on the mounting board. Cover rod with lining fabric as instructed on page 36. Use the spacing of the screw eyes to mark the location of the vertical rows of rings on the rod cover. Tack the rod to the lining side of shade at and just below each of the bottom-most rings, allowing ½ inch of the rod to extend beyond the outside rings.

4. Rig, mount, and dress the shade following the instructions on pages 22 to 26.

RUFFLED BALLOON SHADE ON POLE

*A wooden pole mounts this shade at the window to show off a bias-bound contrast
ruffle that surrounds all four sides of this fancy window dressing.*

MATERIALS

* See Hardware and Notions Checklist, page 25.
* 1¾-inch wood pole and wood pole returns with dowel
  screws
* Extra fabric for ruffles and rosettes
* Contrast fabric for custom-made bias or purchased
  wide bias tape for binding and welt
* ⁵⁄₃₂-inch piping cord

YARDAGE AND CUTTING

1. See the Yardage and Cutting information in Balloon
Shade with Shirr Tape Top (page 54) for the base shade.
Plan two times fullness. The cut length "extra" for the full-
length shade changes to 15 inches and the stationary one to
25 inches.

2. When planning the mounting position for this shade,
note that the ruffle sits above the rod about 3 inches.

3. Plan for the ruffle trim by referring to Creating Ruffles
(opposite). Cut the ruffle strips 7 inches wide for a 3-inch finished ruffle. The ruffles on the side and bottom edges of the
shade are double fullness; the portion that goes across the

top is the cut width of the shade. Allow an extra 12 inches so
you can put extra fullness in the corners of the shade. After
you determine the length of ruffle strip needed for your
shade and whether you want it cut on the straight or bias of
the fabric, plan the cutting layout on paper to determine the
additional yardage needed.

4. Binding is applied to the hem edge of all the ruffles.
The same contrasting fabric will be used to cover piping cord
that will go around the side and bottom edges between the
shade and the ruffles.

5. For the choux rosettes, cut one 14-inch circle for each
rosette, planning one for each row of rings.

6. To create the casing strip for the wood rod, cut a
piece of lining 4½ inches wide by the width of the shade
plus 1¼ inches.

SEWING INSTRUCTIONS
Preparing the Ruffle

1. Cut and seam the strips for the ruffle, joining the ends
to create a circle. Press the strip in half lengthwise, wrong
sides together; baste the raw edges together.

2. Bind the folded edge of the ruffle strip, creating a ½-
inch band, following the instructions under Working with
Bias Binding (page 85).

3. Gather the ruffle strip for application to the sides and
bottom of the shade, leaving the top portion flat.

Constructing the Shade

1. Seam face fabric and lining widths as planned.

2. Make piping as described in Creating and Applying
Piping (page 87), and baste it around the sides and bottom
of the face fabric piece. There is no piping on the top edge.

3. Right sides together, baste the ruffle around all sides
of the face fabric over the piping, crowding extra fabric into
each corner (opposite, top).

4. Right sides together, sew face and lining, leaving an
opening on one edge for turning. Turn right side out; press.

5. On the casing strip, press under ⅝ inch on all edges.
Pin the strip across the top edge of the shade, aligning the
top edge of the strip with the top edge seam line between the
shade and the ruffle. Topstitch the casing strip in place close
to the folded edges (opposite, far right).

6. Mark and sew the rings to the back of the shade as

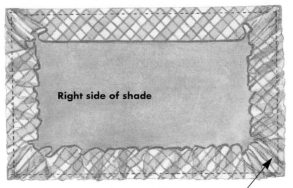

Right side of shade

Crowd extra ruffles into corners.

planned above and following the instructions under Planning and Sewing Rings in Simple Roman Shade (page 34). The first ring at the bottom will be 2 inches above the ruffle seam. Make a mark on the rod casing for the location of each row of rings.

Finishing the Shade

1. Rig the shade according to the instructions on page 26, with these additions:

• The wood pole will serve as the mounting board for this shade. Use the dowel screws to attach the returns to the wood pole.

Determine where on the underside of the wood pole to place the screw eyes, and then drill holes for them.

Slip the shade onto the pole and adjust the gathers.

Align the rows of rings with the screw eye holes. Make a slit in the casing and install the eyes.

• See Balloon Shade with Shirr Tape Top, page 54, for the weight rod information.

2. Make the choux rosettes (page 58). Pin or hand sew them to the rod casing at each row of rings.

3. Mount the shade at the window using the instructions for mounting a pole on pages 25 to 26. Dress the shade as instructed on page 53.

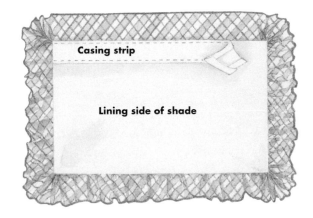

Casing strip

Lining side of shade

Creating Ruffles

Ruffles can lend a feminine air to almost any window covering and are especially effective undulating across a balloon or Austrian shade's hem. To enhance your ruffle savvy, follow these pro tips:

• Use lightweight, drapable fabrics for the softest ruffles.

• Cut ruffling strips on the straight grain to conserve fabric or on the bias to soften a fabric's effect (refer to Working with Bias Binding, beginning on page 85).

• Plan ruffles wide enough and full enough to give your treatment a luxurious look. Most ruffles are between 2 and 4 inches wide when finished and two to three times the length of the edge to be embellished. As a general rule, the wider and sheerer the fabric, the fuller the ruffle should be.

1. For ruffles to be caught in seams, cut strips twice the ruffle finished width, plus 1 inch for seam allowances. Fold the strip in half lengthwise, right sides together, and stitch across each end. Turn the strip to the right side and baste the long raw edges in a 3/8-inch seam.

2. For ruffles to be topstitched, cut strips the finished width of the ruffle, plus 1 inch for hem allowances; press under 1/4 inch twice at all edges and topstitch the hems in place. As an alternative, roll-hem the edges using a conventional machine and rolled hem foot, or a serger adjusted for a rolled hem.

• Gather ruffles to the desired fullness by machine basting a straight stitch or zigzagging over small cording or dental floss, then pulling up the thread. Or use a ruffler attachment on your conventional sewing machine.

• Attach ruffles in one of two ways: Catch them in seams (baste first to the face fabric, right sides together and raw edges even) or topstitch them to the treatment edge through the ruffle's center or upper finished edge.

• Layer multiple ruffles in creative color and print combinations for exciting results.

CASUAL BALLOON SHADE

*This nonchalant window dressing provides a dramatic effect with very easy casing
top construction and curtain rod installation.*

MATERIALS

* See Hardware and Notions Checklist, page 25.
* Spring-tension rod for inside mount or curtain rod for outside mount

YARDAGE AND CUTTING

1. The cut width of the shade is 2 to 2½ times the width of the rod, fullness depending on the weight of the fabric, plus 4 inches for 1-inch double side hems.

2. The cut length is the finished length plus 29 inches. The photographed shade is not a working shade, but it can be made as one by using the instructions in Mounting and Rigging on page 22.

SEWING INSTRUCTIONS

1. Make 1-inch double hems on sides and bottom of shade. The bottom hem will serve as a pocket for the weight rod.

2. To make the top rod casing, press under 2 inches at top edge of shade to the wrong side. Press under ½ inch on the raw edge and stitch the casing in place.

3. Plan and attach rings to the back of the shade based on the instructions for the Simple Roman Shade (page 34). Cover and insert the weight rod in the bottom hem pocket, distributing the gathers evenly. Tack the rod to the pocket at the ends and at each row of rings.

4. For a balloon shade functioning as a valance, tie enough rings together to achieve the desired length; no rigging is necessary. For a working shade, rig it according to the instructions on page 26. For either treatment, mount the shade at the window by inserting a rod through the top casing.

BOX-PLEATED CLOUD SHADE

Pleating the top of a cloud shade creates a more tailored look; the more pleats you add, the fuller your shade will be.

MATERIALS

* See Hardware and Notions Checklist, page 25.
* Mounting board: 1 × 4 inches

YARDAGE AND CUTTING

1. As you plan your shade width, have one pleat at each row of rings and one in the center of each balloon section. The finished space in each balloon section between the rows of rings should not exceed 18 inches. The total of the spaces plus 6 inches should equal the finished width of the shade. For greater fullness, add extra pleats in each section rather than increasing the amount of fabric in each pleat. The shade is mounted on a board that is turned on edge, so that the 3½-inch side is facing into the room and the narrow edge is parallel to the floor. Make appropriate adjustments if you wish more than a 1-inch projection from the wall or if you want to add returns. (See Mounting and Rigging, page 22.)

2. The cut width is the finished width plus 4 inches for each pleat and 6 inches for the side hems.

3. The cut length is the height of the window (or mounting space) plus 3½ inches for mounting board allowance and 2 inches for the bottom hem.

4. Allow extra yardage to cover the mounting board and weight rod with shade fabric.

SEWING INSTRUCTIONS

Constructing the Shade

1. Seam fabric widths if necessary, planning seams at rows of rings.

2. Sew 1½-inch double side hems. Clean-finish the top edge with a serger or purchased binding.

3. At the top edge and 7½ inches down from there, mark off the pleats and spaces as indicated on the diagram. Make the same pleat marks at the hem edge and 3 inches up from there.

4. On the wrong side of the shade, mark the vertical lines for the rings, keeping the rows even and parallel. At the outside edges, the lines should be 5 inches in from the side, at the center of the pleat. The rows in between should be in the center of every other pleat.

5. Mark the ring positions, 5 to 6 inches apart,

along the vertical lines, planning the first ring for the top of the bottom hem. At this point, that will be 2 inches up from the cut edge; it is easier to mark ring positions before making the pleats top and bottom. The last ring at the top must be at least 18 inches down from the top of the shade. Sew the rings to the shade at the marked spots by machine zigzag stitch or by hand, leaving off the very bottom rings until after you have made the pleats.

Making the Pleats

1. Bring together the marks on either side of each pleat; the pleat should be on the face side of the panel. Stitch the pleat from the top of the shade to the mark 7½ inches down, backstitching at both ends. At the hem edge, stitch up 3 inches. Measure the panel to be sure the finished width is correct.

2. Flatten the pleats against the panel, centering them over the stitching line (see page 68). Tack the pleats in place by machine at the top of the top pleats, 3½ inches down from the top, at the bottom of the bottom pleats, and 3 inches up from the bottom. Baste the remaining 4 inches of the top pleats.

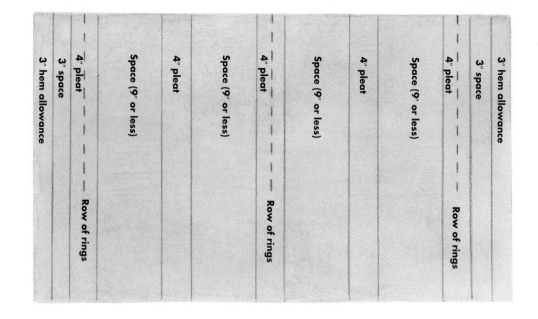

The diagram is labeled (from right to left): 3" hem allowance | 3" space | 4" pleat | Space (9" or less) — Row of rings | 4" pleat | Space (9" or less) | 4" pleat | Space (9" or less) — Row of rings | 4" pleat | Space (9" or less) | 4" pleat | Space (9" or less) — Row of rings | 4" pleat | 3" space | 3" hem allowance

Finishing

1. Turn up 2 inches at the bottom and create a 1-inch double hem. Stitch in place along top folded edge, creating a rod pocket as well as the hem.

2. Cover the mounting board with shade fabric, making sure that the ends have a clean, finished look. Place screw eyes along the narrow edge of the board to align with the rows of rings; the outside ones will be 3 inches in from the end and the rest equally spaced in between.

3. Mark on the shade with pins or soluble ink marker the board edge line, 3½ inches down from the top. Aligning that line with the board edge, staple the shade to the board.

4. Rig and dress the shade according to the instructions on pages 22 to 26. Insert the weight rod, cut to ½ inch less than the finished shade and covered with shade fabric, into the hem/rod pocket. Sew the ends closed. To mount the shade, screw the board directly to the window frame; the area behind the end pleats is a good spot, as the screw head will be hidden by the layers of fabric in the pleat. Remove the pleat basting stitches.

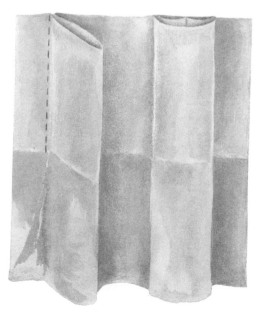

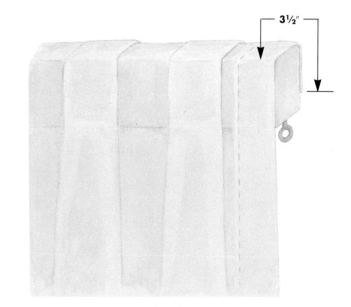

3½"

GOBLET-PLEATED BALLOON SHADE

A bold variation on pinch pleats, the goblet construction creates cup-shaped pleats that can be further enhanced by the addition of a decorative cord knotted at each goblet.

2. The cut width is the finished width plus 4 to 5 inches for each pleat for up to two times fullness. Add 2 inches for the side hems.

3. The cut length is the height of the window (or mounting space) plus 2½ inches.

4. Cut the lining the same as the face fabric, less the 2-inch side hem allowance.

5. For the cord trim, add together the width of the shade, twice the return, 8 inches (¼-inch-diameter) to 10 inches (⅜-inch-diameter) for each knot at a pleat, and ¼ yard for ease and finishing the ends.

SEWING INSTRUCTIONS
Constructing the Shade

1. Seam fabric and lining widths if necessary.

2. Right sides together, pin the face and lining fabrics, aligning all raw edges. Stitch the sides only with ½-inch seams. With wrong sides still out, center the lining on the face fabric, pressing the seams toward the lining. Stitch across the top raw edges with a ½-inch seam.

3. Cut buckram ½ inch narrower than shade panel. With the wrong side of the face fabric up, lay one edge of the buckram across the top of the panel on the seam

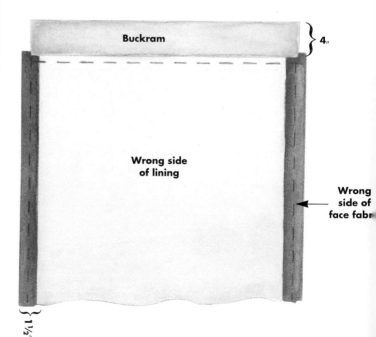

Buckram

4″

Wrong side
of lining

Wrong
side of
face fabr

1½″

MATERIALS

* See Hardware and Notions Checklist, page 25.
* 4-inch-wide buckram
* Hook-and-loop fastener tape
* Twisted cord trim: ¼-inch to ⅜-inch diameter

YARDAGE AND CUTTING

1. Plan one pleat at each row of rings and two equally spaced in between in each balloon section. The finished space between the rows of rings should not exceed 18 inches. This shade is inside-mounted; add space and fabric at the sides of the shade for returns on an outside mount.

allowance and stitch it in place. Turn the panel right side out through the hem edge and press. The buckram lies between the lining and face fabric, and 1½ inches of the face fabric should show on either side of the lining.

4. At the bottom edge, press up 2 inches for hem. Turn under 1 inch to make a 1-inch double hem. Stitch in place close to the upper fold line, making a hem as well as a casing for the weight rod.

5. On the wrong side of the shade, mark the vertical lines for the rings, keeping the rows even and parallel. At the outside edges, the lines should be in from the side edge, 1 inch plus half the amount of fabric in each pleat; the lines should fall in the center of each pleat. The rows in between should be in the center of every other pleat.

6. Mark the ring positions, 5 to 6 inches apart, along the vertical lines, placing the first ring at the top of the bottom hem. The last ring at the top must be at least 18 inches down from the top of the shade. Sew the rings to the shade at the marked spots by machine zigzag stitch or by hand.

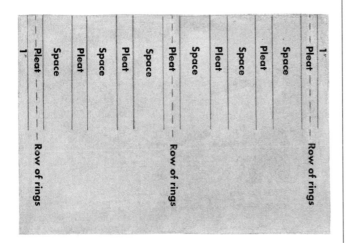

Making the Pleats

1. Plan the pleats and spaces on paper (below).

• From the width of the shade panel subtract the total inches allowed for the pleats.

• From that result, subtract 2 inches for the end spaces.

• Divide the remainder by the number of spaces on your shade to determine the inches in each space.

2. Using pins or soluble ink pen, transfer the paper markings on to the right side of the fabric panel.

3. Make the pleats, working from the wrong side of the panel. Bring together the pins at either side of each pleat so that the pleat is formed on the right side of the panel. At the

pin line and on the face side of the panel, stitch the pleat from the bottom of the buckram to the top of the panel, backstitching at both ends. Measure the panel width to be sure the finished width is correct.

4. Pinch the fabric in each pleat into three sections only at the base of the pleat, not at the top. Tack the pinched area together using a machine zigzag tacking stitch or by hand tacking. Push out the upper section into a cup shape (right).

5. To maintain the goblet shape of the pleat, stuff the opening with fiberfill or scraps of soft fabric such as flannel interlining or batting.

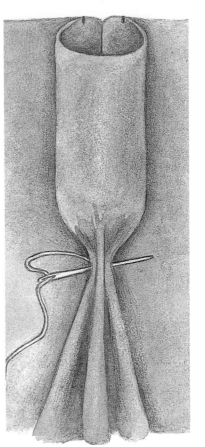

Finishing

1. Hand sew the loop side of the fastener tape to the back of the shade across the pleats, ⅜ inch down from the top edge. Attach the hook side of the tape to the narrow edge of the mounting board.

2. Attach the cord trim to the pleat area of the shade with knots at the base of the goblets. The trim can be sewn on by hand, but the easiest method is to glue it on with a tacky glue, holding the knots in place with pins until the glue is dry. Start at one end of the shade, gluing the cord over to the first pleat. Tie a knot as described in Creating the Perfect Knot, page 60, and glue in place. Glue cord over to the next pleat; tie a knot and glue. Repeat across the shade.

3. Cut the weight rod to ½ inch less than the finished width of the shade. Make a tube of fabric to cover the rod. Instead of finishing the ends as described on page 36, allow extra at the ends to make a "tab." Insert the rod into the hem casing. Tack the rod cover "tabs" to the hem casing at each end. Adjust the gathers on the rod and tack the rod cover to the hem casing at each row of rings.

4. Rig, mount, and dress the shade according to the instructions on pages 22 to 26.

SHEER AUSTRIAN SHADE

Using traditional Austrian shade tape adds lush festooning and more privacy to a sheer fabric; this treatment stands alone or complements drapery panels.

MATERIALS

* See Hardware and Notions Checklist, page 25.
* Austrian shade ring tape or transparent two-cord shirring tape with cross threads (instead of rings)
* Curtain rod with a 1-inch or less return, or ⅜-inch rodding

YARDAGE AND CUTTING

1. Sheer Austrian shades call for a diaphanous type of fabric, such as batiste, ninon, or voile. The fullness of the shade is achieved both vertically from shirring tapes and horizontally from the fabric gathered onto a rod. (Austrian shades made from other fabrics usually have a tailored top and are hung at the window from a mounting board.)

2. Fullness vertically is usually three times the finished length. The cut length will include 3 inches for the bottom hem plus rod pocket allowance, which for a standard curtain rod is 2½ inches (1⅝-inch casing, ⅝-inch turn under, ¼-inch take up). For a header, add two times the desired height. Add an extra 6 inches of fabric to cover the weight rod.

3. To determine the cut width of the shade, decide first the number and finished width of the scallops. Planning the shade on paper helps position seams and allowances correctly.

* Scallops should be 9 to 12 inches wide after being shirred on the rod, and an odd number of scallops is preferred.
* Start by subtracting 2 inches from the finished width of the shade.
* Divide the result by the number of proposed scallops to get the number of inches in each scallop. If the number does not fall between 9 and 12 inches, adjust the number of scallops accordingly.

4. Decide on the horizontal fullness, which can range from 1¼ to 2 times the finished width. The greater the fullness, the deeper the scallops. Sheer fabrics in extra-wide widths, up to 118 inches, may eliminate any seams, but if seaming is necessary, plan seams to fall at a row of rings. The cut width will include 3 inches for side hems.

5. To determine the amount of shade tape needed, multiply the cut length of the shade by the number of rows of rings, plus extra to allow for aligning the rings horizontally. (There will be one more row of rings than there are scallops.)

SEWING INSTRUCTIONS
Constructing the Shade with Tapes

1. Seam fabric panels if needed. Trim seams to ¼ inch and press open. The seams do not need a clean finish, as they will be covered with the shade tape. Press under 1½ inches on each side. Make a double 1½-inch hem at the bottom. At the top edge of the shade, press and pin in a casing, with header if planned, according to instructions for the Sheer Cloud Shade (page 59); do not sew yet.

2. Lay out the shade, wrong side up. Pin a length of shade tape over each side hem, the edge 1 inch in from the folded side edge. Position the first ring 2 inches above the lower edge of the shade. Cut off the tape even with the lower edge of the sheer. At the top edge, allow the tape to extend 1 inch into the casing. Using a zipper foot, stitch these tapes in place, starting 2 inches up from the bottom just above the first ring and always stitching from the bottom to the top (below).

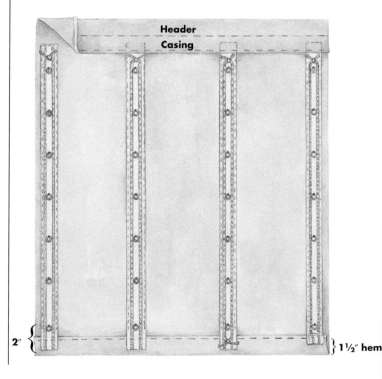

Header

Casing

2″

} 1½″ hem

3. Pin and stitch the rest of the tapes to the sheer in the same manner, positioning them as planned in Yardage and Cutting in Step 4, page 72.

4. To secure the cords at the bottom of the shade, dig out the cords from the tape 1½ inches above the bottom edge and knot them securely; a dab of glue is insurance. At the top edge dig out the cords just below the casing and knot in the same way.

5. To create loops at the bottom of the shade to hold the weight rod, turn up 1¼ inches on each tape. Turn under ½ inch of that allowance to make a loop. (The tied cords will be inside the loop.) By hand, slipstitch the loop closed just under the first ring, sewing through the loop only and not the sheer fabric.

Shirring the Shade

1. One tape at a time, pull the knotted cords at the top of the shade until it has reached the desired finished length. If you can pin the bottom of the shade to a padded surface to keep it straight while you pull the cords, the process will be easier. Retie the cords securely to keep the shirring from slip-

ping and then cut off excess cord. Adjust the gathers.

2. Cut the weight rod 1 inch shorter than the finished width of the shade. Cover it with a tube of a double layer of the sheer fabric. Mark the rod with the finished spacing of the scallops and then insert it through the loops at the bottom of the shade, matching the marks and the centers of the loops. Tack the rod cover to the rod loops to keep the scallops evenly spaced and the rod from shifting.

Mounting and Rigging the Shade

1. Prepare a mounting board with the screw eyes inserted in the narrow edge (⅝ inch) and attach the board with the wide (1½-inch) side against the window frame, or screw the eyes directly into the window framing. Attach the curtain rod. (See Box-Pleated Cloud Shade, page 67, for illustration.)

2. Rig the shade according to the instructions on pages 22 to 26, and then hang it from the curtain rod at the window. Leave enough shade cord at each row of rings to complete the rigging through the screw eyes after the shade is hung at the window.

PLEATED BALLOON SHADE

Balloon shades do not have to be fussy; witness this tailored, yet soft, window dressing with a crisp pleated fabric detailing across the top.

MATERIALS

* See Hardware and Notions Checklist, page 25.

YARDAGE AND CUTTING

1. This balloon shade is flat when lowered, so take the same measurements as you would for a Roman shade. In order to determine the width of each balloon section, divide the finished width measurement by the number of sections desired. The sections can be any width, but 8 to 12 inches is suggested. Consider the position of seams, which should be hidden in pleats, when deciding on the width of each section.

pleated fabric. For a pleated strip 2 inches wide, you will need to cut fabric strips 5 inches wide by three times the length of the board and returns.

SEWING INSTRUCTIONS
Constructing the Shade

1. Seam the face fabric as needed. Following the diagram below, mark off the location of the pleats, fold lines, and the center of the pleat on a 6-inch-wide strip of paper or buckram cut to the width of the shade piece. Transfer these markings to the wrong side of the shade fabric.

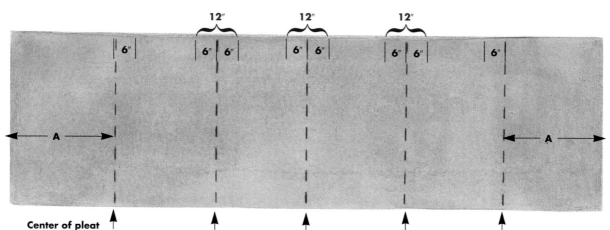

Center of pleat

A=Width of board plus 2-inch hem allowance

The pleat itself usually takes about 12 inches of fabric, but the range is 9 to 12 inches.

2. The cut length of the shade is the finished length plus 19 to 29 inches. Nineteen inches allows for three 5-inch permanent poufs at the bottom of the shade, 2 inches for mounting board allowance, and 2 inches for a hem. The longer the shade, the more ballooning that will occur. (If you use 6-inch spacing between rings, adjust these figures.)

3. The cut width of the shade is the finished width, plus the pleat allowance times the number of pleats, 2 inches for side hems, and twice the depth of the mounting board (outside mount only). The half pleats at each side of the shade count as one.

4. Cut the lining fabric the same length as the face fabric and 2 inches narrower than the *finished* width of the shade.

5. The top of the shade is finished off with a strip of

2. Form the pleats, stitching them together 4 inches up from the bottom and ½ inch more than the mounting board allowance down from the top. Pin or baste the rest of each pleat in place.

3. Seam lining fabric if neeeded. With right sides together, place the lining so that its bottom edge is 2 inches above that of the face fabric. Match the side edges, pin, and sew just those edges together with a ½-inch seam. Turn the shade right side out; ½ inch of face fabric extends on to the back. The back now looks similar to the illustration in the Simple Roman Shade (page 34).

4. At the bottom edge of the shade, make a 1-inch double hem. Sew in place by hand or machine, catching the lining in the hem.

5. At the top of the shade, sew together the face fabric and lining and clean-finish the raw edges.

Planning and Sewing the Rings

1. On the lining side of the shade, mark the location of the center of the pleats with a vertical line for each pleat, including one at each side the distance of the return in from the edge. The outside lines should fall in line with the half-pleat fold on the face of the shade.

2. Mark the ring positions on the vertical lines, placing the first ring at the top of the hem. Space the rings 5 to 6 inches apart, with the last ring 3 inches or more from the top finished line of the shade. Sew the rings at the marked spots through the lining fabric, catching the face fabric at the center back of each pleat.

3. Cut the weight rod ½ inch less than the finished width of the shade, and insert it into the casing created by the bottom hem. The ends of the rod should align with the outside rows of rings. Then fold back the return allowance against the hem and tack it in place.

4. Mount, rig, and dress the shade according to the instructions on pages 22 to 26.

Making the Decorative Pleated Trim

1. Cut and seam the strips of fabric for the pleated top finish, cutting them on the bias if it seems appropriate. Right sides together, sew the long edges of the strip with a ½-inch seam, making a tube. Turn and press with the seam in the center of the strip.

2. Make ⅜-inch pleats across the length of the strip, pressing and pinning the pleats in place as you go. Use the Perfect Pleater™ if you have one (see Resource Guide, page 94). Stitch through the center of the pleats.

3. Glue or tack the pleated strip across the top edge and returns of the shade.

Creating Balloon and Austrian Shades

FESTOON SHADE

This soft shade usually joins simple side hangings. Adding trim to the bottom edge eliminates the need to trim the drapery panels.

MATERIALS

* See Hardware and Notions Checklist, page 25.
* Bullion fringe: 4 inches wide
* Twill tape: 1/2 inch wide by 6 inches long

YARDAGE AND CUTTING

1. This festoon shade, as an under-treatment, should extend at least 6 inches under the panels on either side. Thus the minimum mounting board width is the width of the festoon plus 12 inches. The center of the side pleats should align with the lead edge of the panels.

2. The cut length of the shade is the finished length plus 19 to 29 inches. Nineteen inches allows for three 5-inch permanent poufs at the bottom of the shade, 2 inches for the mounting board allowance, and 2 inches for a hem. To create more ballooning, add more length for more poufs in the shade. (If you use 6-inch spacing between rings, adjust the allowance for the permanent poufs.)

3. The cut width of the shade is the width of the mounting board plus 24 inches for two pleats, one at each side of the center pouf; add 2 inches for side hems.

4. Purchase bullion fringe equal to the cut width of the shade.

SEWING INSTRUCTIONS
Constructing the Shade

1. Decide the width of the festoon section based on the over-treatment. The fabric on each side of the festoon will hang softly to form "butterfly" tails, but will be covered by the draperies.

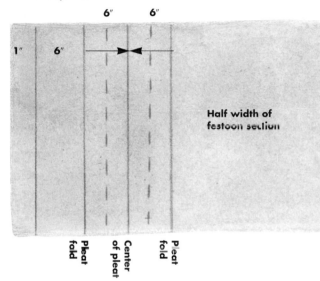

2. Seam the face fabric if needed, being certain that the seams will fall within a pleat. Using the diagram above, mark off the location of the pleats, fold lines, and the center of the pleat on the shade. If you are making more than one shade, you can make these markings on a 6-inch strip of paper or buckram the width of the shade piece. Transfer these markings to the wrong side of the shade fabric.

3. Form the two pleats, stitching them together 4 inches up from the bottom and ½ inch more than the mounting board allowance down from the top. Pin or baste the rest of each pleat in place.

4. Baste the fringe to the bottom edge of the right side of the shade, starting and stopping 1 inch in from each side. The top band of the fringe is aligned with the bottom raw edge of the shade, and the fringe itself extends into the shade. Turn over the raw edges of the fringe so that they will face the wrong side of the shade when it is turned right side out.

5. Cut two pieces of twill tape, each 3 inches long. Slip

the tape through a plastic ring; fold the tape in half to create a loop. Pin the loop with the plastic ring over the fringe, matching the center of the tape to the center of the pleat line and having the raw edges of the tape even with the bottom raw edge of the shade.

6. Seam lining fabric if needed. With right sides together, place the lining so that its bottom edge is aligned with that of the face fabric. Match the side edges, pin, and sew just those edges together with a ½-inch seam; do not sew the bottom or top edges.

7. With the right sides still together, reposition the lining so that it is centered over the face fabric and ½ inch of the face fabric is visible on each side. Pin in place and sew the bottom edges together.

8. Turn the shade right side out and press; ½ inch of the face fabric extends onto the back.

9. At the top of the shade, sew together the face fabric and lining and clean-finish the raw edges.

Planning and Sewing the Rings

1. On the lining side of the shade, mark the location of the center of each of the pleats by drawing a vertical line.

2. Mark the ring positions on the vertical lines. The first ring is already on the twill tape loop. Measuring from the seam line where the tape is attached (not from the ring), space the other rings 5 to 6 inches apart, with the last ring 3 inches or more down from the top finished line of the shade. Sew the rings at the marked spots through the lining fabric, catching the face fabric at the center back of each pleat.

3. Cut the weight rod 3 inches longer than the center festoon, and cover it with lining fabric as described on page 36. Slip the covered rod through the twill tape loops, allowing the rod to extend 1½ inches out each side from the center of the tape. Tack the rod cover to the loops.

4. Mount, rig, and dress the shade according to the instructions on pages 22 to 26.

For inspiration and information on creating companion drapery panels, refer to *Make It with Style: Draperies & Swags*.

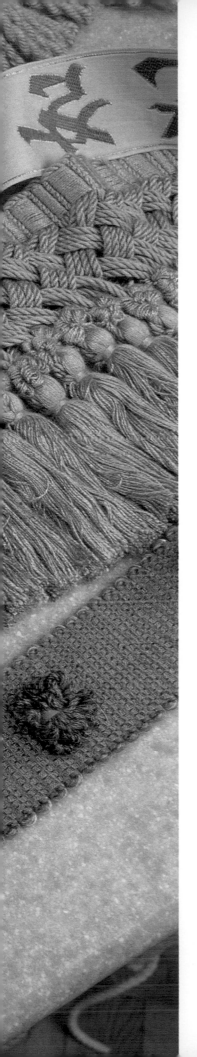

Tools, Terms, and Techniques

Here's where you'll find information and resource materials to assist you in making the most professional window shades possible. Learn how to create a mounting board—without handyman credentials. Whether you plan to mount inside or outside the window, on a wooden pole or under an upholstered cornice, the directions are here for you. Adding end covers to your outside mounting board will give the finished look you love. Making trims to enhance your window shades will be simple following instructions on working with bias, binding edges, and creating custom piping. The glossaries will clarify any terms you encounter in this book that are unfamiliar, guiding you through Fabrics and Fibers, Hardware and Notions, Decorative Trims, as well as Terms and Techniques used to create your window shades.

Making an Upholstered Cornice

Enhance panels or valance and panel combinations with decorative cornices you make yourself. These lovely structures add regal elegance to even the most basic windows. The construction and installation of these wood boxes—minus a back and bottom—involve basic woodworking skills. Cover them by tautly stapling fabric in place over batting, or simply paint them and embellish as desired. If appropriate, mount the traverse rod for an under-treatment to the top board underside.

Materials

- Lumber: 1-inch (actually about ¾-inch-thick) No. 2 kiln-dried pine
- Nails and/or angle irons
- Fabric
- Batting
- Staple gun and ⁵⁄₁₆-inch to ½-inch staples
- Lining fabric or paint (optional)
- Fabric glue (optional)
- Push pins (optional)

Planning

1. You'll need four wood pieces to create the cornice. The face board is cut to the desired finished cornice width by the desired finished height. The top board is cut twice the wood thickness shorter than the face board with the same depth as the leg board. The two leg boards are cut the desired cornice projection from the wall minus the wood thickness by the cornice height.

2. Unless the fabric has a directional pattern, it is preferable to railroad the fabric to avoid seaming and to save yardage. To determine any fabric yardage requirements: Add together the cornice width, twice the return (leg board depth) and 6 inches (for wrapping) to calculate the fabric width; add 6 inches to the cornice height to calculate the fabric length. The top board may be covered with the same fabric or lining fabric, or may be painted. If you plan to cover the top board with fabric or lining, add 6 inches to each top board dimension to determine the (additional) yardage required.

3. To determine the batting yardage required: Measure the constructed wood cornice from leg back edge to leg back edge over the face board to calculate the width; add 2 inches to the face board upper-to-lower-edge measurement to calculate the length.

4. You'll need approximately eight angle irons for a standard cornice; however, if your cornice is extra-wide or very heavy, use an extra angle iron at each joint and on each surface that mounts to the wall. Also, you may substitute nails for the angle irons joining the face board to the leg boards.

Construction

1. Measure and cut the boards in the dimensions determined, checking that all boards are perfectly square.

2. Using angle irons or nails, attach the leg boards to the back edges of the face board.

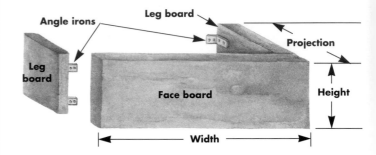

3. Cover the cornice face and legs with batting, bringing the batting over the upper and lower edges and just slightly to the back sides. Glue or staple the batting in place.

4. Center the fabric right-side-out over the face board. If desired, use push pins to temporarily hold the fabric in place. Beginning at the centers, pull the fabric around the face board upper and lower edges to the board back and staple it in place, pulling the fabric taut over the batting.

5. Repeat Step 4 to staple the fabric to each leg board upper and lower edge, then the leg board back edges, trimming and mitering the corners for a smooth finish.

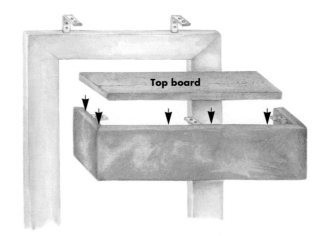

6. Cover the top board with fabric only or paint it and let it dry. Slip the completed top board between the leg boards at the face board upper edge and secure it at the underside with angle irons.

7. Mount the cornice to the wall using angle irons.

Making a Mounting Board

This do-it-yourself hardware forms a stable structure for mounting lovely valances, swags, and jabots. Even if you're not especially handy, you can create your own without much experience. Refer to Pre-Mounting Planning on page 24 and Mounting Tips and Tricks on page 26 for more guidelines on size and usage of mounting boards.

Materials
- Lumber: 1-inch (actually about ¾-inch-thick) No. 2 kiln-dried pine (see below)
- Angle irons
- Lining fabric or paint
- Staple gun and ⁵⁄₁₆-inch to ½-inch staples or hook portion of hook-and-loop fastener tape

Planning

1. You'll need one piece of wood the desired treatment finished width by the necessary depth. If the mounting board is for a valance or swag-and-jabot treatment that will have an under-treatment, cut the board 2 inches longer and 2 inches deeper than the under-treatment. If the mounting board will be used for an inside-mounted swag and jabot, cut it ¼ inch shorter than the treatment desired width.

2. To cover the board with lining fabric, add 6 inches to each board dimension to determine the required yardage.

3. You'll need two angle irons to mount boards for treatments up to 36 inches. Add another angle iron for each additional 18 to 30 inches in width, depending on the weight of the treatment.

Construction

1. Center the board face down on the fabric wrong side; pull and staple the fabric to the wrong side, beginning at each side center and trimming and mitering corners as needed. The stapled side will be the upper side.

2. If using a hook-and-loop tape application, staple the hook portion of the tape to the board as desired.

3. For an inside mount, screw the board directly into the top of the window frame or secure it with angle irons into the frame sides.

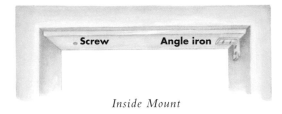

Inside Mount

For an outside mount, use angle irons to secure the board above the window, either on the frame or well above it.

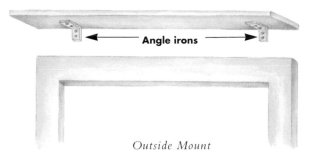

Outside Mount

Mounting a Pole with Angle Irons

- Choose the size (leg measurement) of the angle irons based on the desired return depth of the window treatment.

- Position the angle irons on the wall or window frame, keeping in mind that the pole will sit on top of the angle irons.

- Plan an angle iron within 3 inches from each end of the pole. If the span between those end angle irons is greater than 40 inches, plan a keyhole support bracket in the middle of that span.

- Mount the angle irons on the wall as planned. Lay the rod, with or without the window treatment mounted on it, on top of them and mark the location for the screws. Make pilot holes in the rod. If you then put the window treatment on the pole, be certain that those pilot holes face downward. Then reposition the rod on the angle irons and screw up through the holes in the angle irons, through the fabric into the pole.

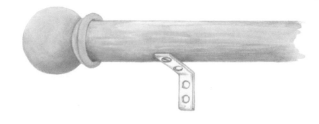

Making Mounting Board End Covers

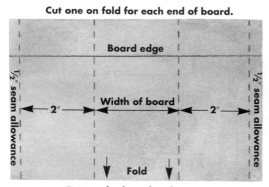

Cut one on fold for each end of board.

Board edge

½" seam allowance

← 2" → **Width of board** ← 2" →

½" seam allowance

↓ **Fold** ↓

Pattern for board end covers

- Before mounting the shade treatment on the board, staple the covers to each end of it, aligning the board edge line on the cover with the board edge and centering the cover over the end of the board.

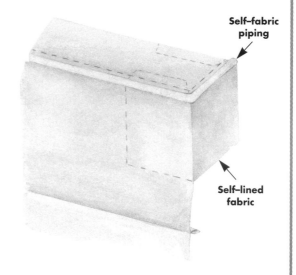

Self–fabric piping

Self–lined fabric

- If your outside-mounted shade treatment has no return, conceal the screw eyes and cord rigging that can be seen from the side view with a self-fabric board end cover.

- Cut out two board end cover patterns from the fabric.

- Fold each piece along the fold line, right sides together. Sew the ends. Turn and press.

How to Apply Trim

There are four basic methods of application, depending on the type and weight of the trim, its potential lifespan, and your preference. Always test your application choice before making a final decision, and start by marking your placement lines using a water- or air-soluble marker.

- **SEWING BY HAND.** Because of the beautiful, pucker-free result it offers, this time-honored (and often time-consuming) method is still the mode of choice for applying heavy or elaborate trims or expensive trims you may want to remove and reuse in the future.

Trim In-Seam Application

Fringe and cord with lip are both well suited to being caught in seams, creating a polished, sophisticated finish.

To insert fringe in a seam

1. Leave intact any temporary chain stitching holding the fringe together. If the fringe doesn't have any chain stitching, carefully secure the fringe with masking or transparent tape (test first to be sure the tape won't harm the fringe) to keep it from moving about and getting caught in the seam.

2. Position the fringe heading completely within the seam allowance so none of it will show on the completed treatment; baste the fringe heading in place just above the lower edge of the heading.

3. During the construction of the window treatment, plan your stitching so it falls within the fringe, just below the lower edge of the heading.

4. Remove chain stitching, any tape, and basted stitches to complete.

To insert cord with lip in a seam

1. Position the lip completely within the seam allowance so none of it will show on the completed treatment; using a zipper foot, baste the lip in place just above its lower edge.

2. During the construction of the window treatment, plan your stitching so it falls at the point where the cord joins the lip. Remove basted stitches.

- To stitch from the wrong side, use a short running stitch along each trim long edge.
- To stitch from the right side, use a slip-baste or blind stitch along each trim long edge.

- **SEWING BY MACHINE.** Use this method for light- to medium-weight trims that are flat, have flat edgings, or feature a channel for stitching along. For the best results, choose trims in weights compatible with the fabric weight, use basting tape or glue stick to adhere the trim in place before stitching (test first), and use nonwoven tear-away stabilizer beneath the project. If puckering is a problem, change your stitch length, loosen the stitch tension, or change to a larger needle. When sewing multiple rows, stitch them all in the same direction to avoid twisting.

- Attach all but the narrowest flat trims with two straight edges—such as ribbon, gimp, and middy braid—by edge-stitching them in place on the right side of the treatment panels before construction and hemming. This method also works well for attaching the flat heading portion of fringe, as long as the thickness allows. Also refer to Mitering Flat Trims, page 35, for instructions on applying flat trims to corners.

- Secure narrow or irregular-edged trims, such as soutache, rickrack, or narrow ribbon, by topstitching them in place using a single row of straight stitching down the center. Use a narrow zigzag to couch narrow cording in place.

- Insert cord with lip or ruffling in a seam, by first machine basting the trim lip or upper edge allowance in place, then catching the trim in seams during construction.

- Apply bias binding by machine stitching, referring to the complete instructions on page 85, unless multiple thicknesses require you to do the work by hand.

- **FUSING.** Innovations in fusibles offer us more no-sew options every day. Available on rolls in a variety of widths ranging from $1/4$ inch to $7/8$ inch (choose one slightly narrower than your trim), webs and adhesives with peel-away backing allow you to first adhere the fusible to the trim, then fuse the trim as desired on the treatment; the heat of your iron does all of the work. Fusing is most appropriate on lighter-weight and less expensive trims.

- **GLUING.** This easy method uses fabric or tacky craft glues to adhere trims in place for a pucker-free result. Most of these glues allow dry cleaning, and some, if not water-soluble, allow washing as well. Like fusing, this method is best suited to lighter-weight and less expensive trims.

Little details like attractively finished trim ends are hallmarks of a custom look. Some finishes may take a little extra time, but they aren't difficult.

To Finish Fringe and Flat Trim Ends

1. Allow an extra 2 inches of trim for each side to be finished.

2. At the beginning and end of the application, turn under 1 inch so the trim is even with the treatment corner or butts the other trim end.

3. For top-applied trims, edgestitch across each end; for in-seam applications, baste each end in place and, when catching the trim in a seam during the construction of the treatment, stitch carefully over the extra bulk.

To Finish Cord or Cord with Lip Ends Using the Flush Method

1. Allow an extra $\frac{1}{2}$ inch of trim for each treatment edge. Baste the trim in place, leaving $\frac{1}{2}$ inch unstitched and $\frac{1}{4}$ inch extending beyond the edge at each end.

2. If using cord with lip, snip the thread attaching the lip to the cord from the cord end to the treatment edge;

trim away the lip flush with the treatment edge.

3. Wrap each trim end for $\frac{1}{2}$ inch with transparent tape. Cut away the excess trim flush with the treatment edge through the tape. Dab some glue on each cord end.

4. If the ends will show, wrap them with matching sewing thread (below).

5. Tack or glue each end in place.

To Finish Cord or Cord with Lip Ends Using the Unravel and Tack Method

1. Allow an extra 3 inches of cord for each treatment edge. Baste the trim in place, leaving $1\frac{1}{2}$ inches at each end unstitched and extending beyond the treatment end.

2. If using cord with lip, snip the thread attaching the lip to the cord from the trim end to the treatment edge.

3. Wrap the cord with transparent tape just beyond each treatment edge.

4. Unravel the cord plies and wrap each ply end with transparent tape.

5. Tack the cord end plies at the treatment's wrong side. If using cord with lip, also tack the lip at the treatment's wrong side (bottom).

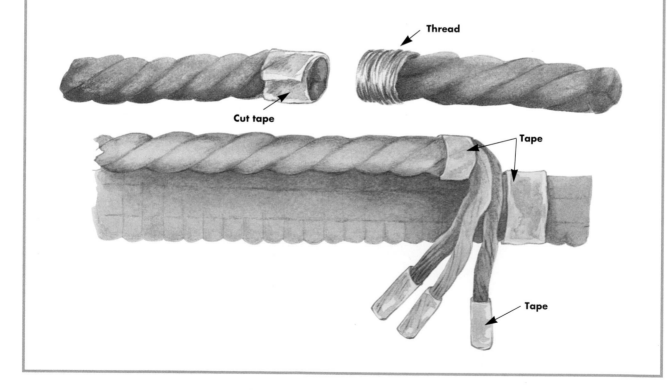

Thread

Cut tape

Tape

Tape

Working with Bias Binding

Enclosing window treatment edges with bias binding can offer beauty—by adding an accent color and line definition—and practicality, by eliminating the need for hems. Use purchased, pre-packaged bias or decorative tape, but for a custom look, or if you need a large quantity, it is an easy matter to make your own.

Cutting Bias Strips and Figuring Yardages

1. Plan to cut the strips four times the finished width you desire, plus $\frac{1}{4}$ inch. To keep seaming to a minimum, purchase at least 1 to $1\frac{1}{2}$ yards of fabric to make bias strips. One yard of 48-inch-wide fabric will yield about 20 yards of $1\frac{5}{8}$-inch-wide strips (piping size) or about 9 yards of $2\frac{1}{4}$-inch-wide strips ($\frac{1}{2}$-inch binding size).

2. Fold the fabric diagonally so the lengthwise grain aligns with the crosswise grain. Press, then cut off the triangle along this fold.

3. Measure and mark lines parallel to the cut edge, spacing them the desired bias width until you have as much as you need. If you have a rotary cutter, mat, and ruler, use them to speed the cutting process. Mark $\frac{1}{4}$-inch seam allowances along the lengthwise grain.

4. Join the strips into a continuous length, with right sides together; align two strips at right angles, matching seam lines. Stitch and press the seams open. Trim off the extending points.

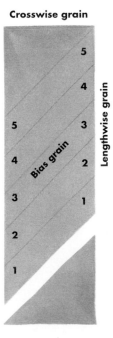

Crosswise grain

Binding an Edge

Choose the method best suited to your fabric weight and skill level:

Method A: French Binding ("Stitch-in-the-Ditch") Application

1. Open out one fold of the binding and pin in place, aligning the crease line to the fabric seam line, right sides together. Stitch along the crease line.

2. Leave the fabric seam allowance untrimmed or trim it to just less than the finished width so that when the binding is turned back over the seam, it will be filled for a lightly puffed, firmer appearance.

3. Bring the binding around to the wrong side, encasing the raw edge(s). Pin the binding in place so the other folded edge covers the previous stitching by at least $\frac{1}{8}$ inch.

4. From the fabric right side, "stitch-in-the-ditch" (the groove created where the binding joins the fabric), being sure to catch the binding on the wrong side.

Method B: Hand-Finished Application

Follow Steps 1 to 3 of Method A, then pin the binding in place so the other folded edge just covers the previous stitching. Stitch in place by hand.

Method C: Topstitched Application

Follow Steps 1 to 3 of Method A, but start the binding application with the right side of the binding to the wrong side of the fabric. Bring the binding over to the right side and topstitch it in place along the folded edge. While you may be tempted to apply the binding with a single row of topstitching, this two-step application will reduce puckering and other problems—and likely save time in the long run.

Finishing Binding Ends

1. Apply the first edge of the binding to the fabric, extending the binding ¾ inch beyond the fabric edge. Trim the fabric seam allowance at the corner on the diagonal.

2. Fold the extending end of the binding back onto itself, then fold the binding down over the fabric edge and complete the application, pivoting to sew across the open end.

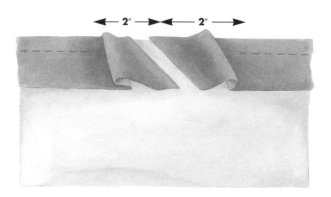

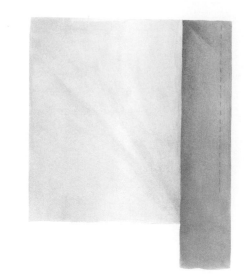

3. Fold the binding toward the right, creating a diagonal fold from the upper left to the lower right corner.

Joining Binding Ends

1. To seam binding ends, start the binding application 2 inches from the beginning point, allowing an extra 1½ inches of binding. Stop the binding application 2 inches from the other side of the beginning point, also allowing an extra 1½ inches of binding.

2. Trim the binding ends on a diagonal, leaving ½-inch seam allowances on each end, and stitch them, right sides together.

3. Press the seams open and continue stitching the binding in place.

4. Fold the binding straight back onto itself toward the left so the binding fold is parallel to the previous stitching line and even with the second fabric raw edge.

Binding Outward Corners

1. Starting on the least conspicuous edge and with the right sides together, sew the binding strip raw edge to one fabric raw edge. (If you are using purchased bias tape, open out one fold of the tape and align the tape fold line with the fabric seam line.)

2. Stop sewing the width of the seam allowance from the corner and backstitch. Raise the needle, lift the presser foot, and, without cutting the threads, pull the fabric to the left of the machine.

5. Pivot the fabric and begin stitching along the adjacent edge, pulling the uncut thread loop to the back.

6. Repeat at all corners and join the ends if applicable.

7. Bring the binding around to the wrong side, encasing the raw edge(s) and turning under the binding seam allowance.

8. Pin the binding in place on the wrong side, folding a miter in the binding at the corners. To distribute the bulk, fold the binding on the back in the opposite direction of that on the front. Finish, using the method chosen under Binding an Edge, page 85.

Creating and Applying Piping

To define or finish seams and edges, or to add an understated decorative touch, piping works best. Purchase this fabric-wrapped cord or make it yourself, starting with cotton or polyester cord (available in $\frac{1}{8}$-inch to 1-inch diameters) and strips cut from the desired fabric. Refer to Working with Bias on page 85 for instructions on planning, cutting, and joining bias strips, ideal for all edges and a must for curved ones. A rotary cutter, mat, and ruler make the cutting job easy, quick, and accurate. Cut straight-grain strips for use only on straight edges.

To Create Piping

1. Wrap the strip, right side out, around the cord so the raw edges are even.

2. Using a zipper foot positioned to the right of the needle, stitch next to the cord, but do not crowd it.

To Apply Piping

1. Position the piping on a window treatment panel (usually on the face fabric), raw edges even, and baste it in place over the piping stitching.

2. When catching the piping in a seam, sandwich the piping between the layers and stitch as close as possible to the piping.

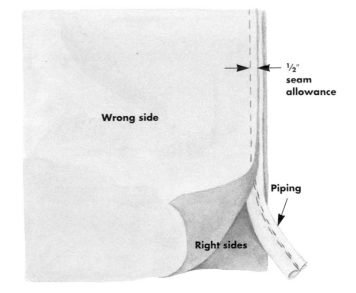

$\frac{1}{2}$" seam allowance

Wrong side

Piping

Right sides

Glossaries

Fabrics and Fibers

Acetate Man-made fiber derived from cellulose acetate; fabrics have luxurious soft feel, silk-like appearance, and excellent draping qualities. Used in such fabrics as taffeta, faille, lace, satin, and crepe; may be combined with other fibers. Fabrics may wrinkle, but they resist stretching and shrinkage. Acetate dyes well, although some dyes will fade. Fabrics usually are dry cleaned.

Acrylic Generic term for synthetic textile fiber resembling wool; acrylic fabrics available in variety of weights, from sheer, wool-like voiles and medium-weight flannels to heavy canvas constructions and pile fabrics. Acrylics resist wrinkles, retain their shape, and are lightweight, strong, colorfast, and moth- and sun-resistant. Fabrics often can be washed following fabric-care labels and require little or no ironing.

Barkcloth Woven drapery fabric with rough or bark-like appearance.

Batiste Soft, sheer, plain-weave fabric, usually in white or pastel color range; can be woven of cotton, silk, linen, wool, or synthetic fibers and blends.

Border print Design engineered along one or both selvages; can be railroaded for special effects.

Broadcloth Densely textured cloth with plain or twill weave and lustrous finish; may be woven in cotton, silk, wool, or synthetic fibers.

Burlap Coarsely woven cloth made of jute, flax, or hemp fibers.

Burn-out Sheer patterned curtain-weight fabric created by chemically "burning out" design, leaving more dense areas floating on less dense ground.

Butcher's linen Coarse, homespun linen-weave cloth originally used for French butcher's smocks, now imitated in many man-made fiber fabrics.

Calico Plain-weave, lightweight fabric similar to percale, printed with small figures; originally woven in all cotton, today often blend of polyester and cotton.

Canvas Heavy, strong, firmly woven cotton, linen, or synthetic fabric; may be soft-finished or highly sized.

Challis Soft, supple, lightweight fabric usually printed with delicate cravat floral or Persian pattern; may be woven of wool, rayon, cotton, or blend.

Chambray Fine-quality plain-weave fabric with linenlike finish, combining colored warp and white filling yarns; woven in solids, stripes, and checks or patterned with jacquard designs.

Chenille Fabric woven with tufted, velvety pile yarns similar in appearance to fuzzy caterpillars.

China silk Plain-weave silk fabric of various weights.

Chintz Plain-weave cotton fabric with glazed surface in solid colors or prints.

Cotton Fibrous, downy, soft substance obtained from seed pods of the cotton plant and spun into yarn, then woven into textiles; used in weaving such cloths as organdy, broadcloth, poplin, and corduroy. Fabrics are strong, comfortable, absorbent, and static-free and dye well, but tend to wrinkle, deteriorate from mildew, and shrink badly if untreated.

Damask Fabric woven on jacquard loom to produce figured designs by combining different weave patterns; damask patterns often utilize satin weave in areas of pattern against plain or twill background so light reflects from fabric.

Dotted Swiss Fine, sheer cotton fabric with embroidered dot pattern and crisp, stiff finish; nylon and polyester/cotton blends also imitate look.

Dupion Fabric woven of slubbed, uneven, double silk threads produced when two cocoons nest together.

Eyelet embroidery Lightweight fabric characterized by small cutout areas with decorative stitching around them to form design; also called broderie anglaise.

Faille One of grosgrain family of cross-rib fabrics often woven of silk, cotton, or synthetic fibers; characterized by light, flat cords usually soft and somewhat glossy.

Fiberglass Fabric constructed from glass in its fibrous form; inherently flame-retardant.

Flannel Soft fabric of plain or twill weave with slightly napped surface on one or both sides; double-faced varieties often used as interlinings.

Flax Soft, silky fiber obtained from bark of flax plant; processed and used in manufacture of linen.

Gabardine Firm, tightly woven fabric with close diagonal twill-weave surface and flat back; may be woven of wool, cotton, or synthetic blends. Usually piece-dyed and finished with high sheen.

Galloon Lace or embroidered fabric with both sides finished with decorative edge design.

Gauze Sheer, thin, open-weave fabric similar to cheesecloth; sometimes finished with stiff sizing.

Georgette Sheer, dull-textured fabric with pebbled or crinkly crepe surface; heavier than chiffon.

Gingham Firm, plain-weave, light- to medium-weight fabric woven into checks, plaids, or stripes; originally made of yarn-dyed cotton, now often woven from polyester/cotton blend. Also refers to traditional check pattern woven of wool, silk, or other fibers.

Herringbone Broken, irregular twill weave creating zigzag effect like herring backbone by alternating direction of twill.

Homespun Originally a general term for cloth hand-woven at home instead of at mill; today refers to coarse fabric of jute, silk, linen, cotton, or blends, generally in plain colors or checked patterns.

Hopsacking Rough-surfaced cotton, linen, or rayon fabric characterized by plain basketweave pattern.

Interlining Fabric layer, usually flannel, sandwiched between face fabric and lining; creates thicker, softer look, giving greater depth and body to treatment. Also prevents bleeding of color and pattern and provides extra layer of insulation.

Jacquard Complex loom with versatile pattern-making mechanism for weaving elaborate designs on fabrics such as damask and brocade.

Lace Fine, openwork fabric with patterns of knotted, twisted, or looped threads on a ground of net or mesh.

Lawn Lightweight, sheer cloth of combed or carded cotton, linen, or cotton blend with crisp finish; may be woven with plissé effect or satin-stripe designs.

Linen Natural strong, lustrous, absorbent fiber removed from stem of flax plant; woven into fabrics from sheer handkerchief weights to heavy, coarse weaves. Usually imported from Ireland or Belgium.

Lining Fabric used for backing window treatments to give richer appearance; may be treated to be resistant to sunlight deterioration, shrinkage, and moisture damage. Most common types are regular, insulated, thermal, and blackout.

Matelassé Patterned fabric with raised woven designs loomed on jacquard machine; surface appears quilted or puckered.

Moiré Fabric with irregular water ripple finish on corded or ribbed weave produced by engraved rollers, steam, heat, or chemicals; usually made of silk, cotton, or rayon.

Mousseline Lightweight, muslinlike cotton with crisp finish closely woven of highly twisted yarns; name ordinarily used in combination with fiber names, as in mousseline de soie.

Muslin Wide variety of plain-weave cotton fabrics ranging from sheer to heavy sheeting; can be unbleached, bleached, dyed in solid colors, or printed.

Ninon A sheer, crisp, smooth fabric of hand-twisted yarns in plain or open weaves; often called triple voile.

Nylon Generic name for man-made polyamide yarns or fibers; range of nylon types produces wide variety of fabric textures, from smooth and crisp to soft and bulky. Often blended with other fibers. Strong, elastic, and resilient, highly resistant to mildew and moths; does not soil easily, but may pill. Washes easily and requires little if any ironing with a cool iron.

Organdy Very fine, sheer, transparent cotton cloth with crisp finish; woven of tightly twisted yarns.

Organza Fine, crisp, transparent silk organdy.

Osnaburg Rough, coarse fabric originally made of flax and named after town in Germany; today is plain-weave coarse cotton of loose, but durable, construction that can be of medium to heavy weight. Often used in unbleached state.

Ottoman Heavyweight fabric with pronounced crosswise rounded ribs, often padded; similar to faille or bengaline, but has heavier ribs.

Peau de Soie French term meaning "skin of silk" for soft, closely woven satin with mellow luster; originally made of silk, may now be made of synthetic fibers.

Percale Fine, lightweight, plain-weave cotton or cotton-blend fabric with firm, balanced construction caused by equal number of threads per inch in warp and weft.

Pima cotton High-quality, long-staple cotton fiber developed from Egyptian cotton seed and originally grown in Pima, Arizona, but now also grown in other western states; used for fine combed cottons and often mercerized.

Piqué Dobby-weave fabric with raised lengthwise cords, welts, or wales in variety of plain or patterned effects.

Plaid Pattern created by colored stripes or bars crossing each other at right angles.

Plissé Thin cotton fabric, soft or crisp, with puckered stripes or patterns in allover blister effect; texture obtained either by weaving with yarns having different degrees of shrinkage in finishing or by chemical treatment.

Polished cotton Cotton fabric with shiny surface achieved either through satin weave or waxed finish.

Polyester Generic term for synthetic fiber with superior properties of wrinkle resistance and easy care; available in many weights, textures, and weaves and often blended with other fibers for minimum-care, durable-press fabrics. Generally washable, quick-drying, and resistant to stretching, shrinking, mildew, and moths. May yellow, but otherwise colorfast; may pill and pick up lint.

Pongee Plain-weave, light- to medium-weight fabric made from wild silk; usually natural, pale, or dark tan color.

Poplin Plain-weave fabric with fine rib running from selvage to selvage; similar to cotton or rayon broadcloth, but has slightly heavier rib. May be woven of silk, cotton, rayon, wool, or blends.

Quilted Layers of fabric padded with soft substance and stitched together by hand or machine with ornamental patterns or crossed lines.

Raw silk Silk fibers as taken from cocoon, before natural gum is removed.

Rayon Generic term for man-made fibers, monofilaments, and continuous filaments made from modified cellulose (wood pulp or cotton fibers too short to spin into yarns); used in a wide range of fabrics, from lightweight to heavy construction. Can resemble natural fibers, has soft hand, and drapes well. Dyes well and usually is colorfast, but has low resistance to mildew and relatively low strength; even weaker when wet. Wrinkles unless specially finished and may shrink or stretch if not treated. Usually dry-cleaned because of low moisture tolerance.

Sailcloth Heavy, strong, extremely durable plain-weave canvas fabric woven of cotton, linen, synthetics, or blends; woven in plain or rib weaves in various weights. Also called duck.

Sateen Cotton fabric characterized by satin weave; usually mercerized and treated to create high luster and crease resistance.

Satin Smooth fabric of silk, cotton, rayon, acetate, or wool with warp threads floated to surface to give lustrous face finish.

Seersucker Lightweight cotton or cotton-blend fabric with crinkled stripes woven in warp direction by holding some yarns under tighter and others under looser tension.

Shantung Plain silk weave characterized by rough, slubbed surface caused by knots and slubs in filling yarns. Today made of silk, cotton, wool, or man-made fibers.

Silk Continuous protein filament produced by larvae of silkworms building cocoons; filament reeled off and boiled to remove stiff natural glue and woven into strong fabrics with soft luster and luxurious hand. Available in a variety of weights and weaves, from sheer chiffon to pongee, heavy tweeds, and brocades. Wrinkle-resistant, exceptionally strong for fineness, very mildew and moth resistant, and dyes well, but may bleed.

Is weakened by sunlight. Usually dry-cleaned.

Suede cloth Woven or knitted fabric of cotton, synthetics, wool, or blends, finished to resemble suede leather.

Taffeta Basic group of plain-weave fabrics smooth on both sides, crisp and usually lustrous. May be plain; woven with fine rib; woven in checks, stripes, or plaids; printed; or woven with uneven threads to create antique taffeta. Weights vary from paper-thin to heavy.

Tartan Woolen or worsted twill fabric woven with colored lines or stripes at right angles to form plaid design.

Tattersall Plaid or check design of dark lines over light ground.

Toile de Jouy A pastoral or historical pattern, often featuring scenery and people, printed in a single color on cotton or linen fabric.

Tussah Silk or durable fabric woven from silkworms, or synthetic imitations.

Twill Fabric woven to produce diagonal ribs or lines on surface.

Velvet Luxurious fabric with low, dense pile on one side; made of silk, rayon, nylon, or polyester.

Velveteen Cotton or synthetic soft, cut-pile fabric; made on woven background with extra set of filling yarns.

Voile Fine, sheer, lightweight plain or printed fabric; fiber content may be cotton, wool, silk, or rayon.

Wool Soft, curly-haired fibers (fleece) with natural felting ability taken from animals such as sheep, angora, cashmere goats, and llamas.

Hardware and Notions

Angle iron L-shaped mounting hardware used for joining mounting board or wood pole to wall or window surface.

Austrian shade ring tape Shirring tape with pre-spaced plastic rings attached; used in making Austrian shades or curtains.

Awning cleat Small device attached to side of window frame for wrapping and securing cords of a fabric shade.

Basting tape Double-sided temporary adhesive tape used to hold fabrics together, instead of or in combination with pins.

Batting Layer of lightweight, lofty cotton or polyester nonwoven material used to wrap, back, or pad a surface; buy the type sold off bolt for more uniform thickness.

Bias binding Prepackaged or self-made fabric strips cut on the bias for use as casings, facings, and decorative trimming.

Cord drops Decorative coverings for ends of shade lift cords; available in weighted and nonweighted styles.

Cording (or piping cord or welting cord) Cotton, polyester, or cellulose fibers held together by open tubular covering used as base for making piping (welting); available in diameters from $5/32$ inch to 2 inches.

Cornice Boxed wood structure, often padded and covered with decorative fabric or painted; mounted alone or over soft window treatment at window upper edge.

Curtain rod Narrow, flat metal rod used for rod-pocket shades, curtains, and valances; available in clear or white.

Fabric dressing Spray-on product used to help shape folds and remove wrinkles and creases, especially after window treatment installation; available from drapery supply businesses (refer to Resource Guide, beginning on page 94).

Fabric glue Tacky, fast-drying glues, especially formulated for bonding fabric and trims; must be clear, flexible, washable, and dry-cleanable.

Finial Attachment placed at each end of curtain rod as ring stop and decorative accent; also sometimes used as embellishment at ends of mounting board.

Fusible web Meltable webs made of synthetic fibers used to bond fabrics together or trim to fabric using iron's heat; available in wide range of widths and types.

Grommets or eyelets Metal hole reinforcements for fabric in sizes ranging from $1/8$ inch to $1/2$ inch in diameter; applied using setting tool kit.

Hollow wall fasteners Special fasteners used to fasten window treatment hardware to wall where no studs are available for anchoring; types include (in ascending order of holding power): plastic expansion anchors, molly screw anchors, and toggle bolts.

Hook-and-loop fastener Two-part sew-on or adhesive-backed fastening product with rough hook side (ideal for attaching to mounting boards) that firmly grasps softer loop side (can be sewn to treatment to be board-mounted); used instead of stapling for fast mounting and laundering ease.

Inside mount Window treatment positioned just inside the window frame; suitable only for windows with 1-inch or greater recess.

Invisible thread Super-fine (.004-mm) soft nylon thread useful for "invisible" topstitching on multicolor fabrics and trims, but not recommended for high-stress areas; available in clear and smoke.

Mounting board or cap board Painted or fabric-covered board secured to wall or window frame with angle irons. The window treatment board mounts to the top of the board or to the edges with staples or hook-and-loop fastener. Traverse rod may hang from underside of board.

Rings Small circles made of plastic, metal, or other materials used to guide draw cords of a fabric shade or to secure tiebacks to wall.

Roman shade tape Twill tape with prespaced plastic rings sewn to tape; tape is sewn to back of shade and cord is threaded through rings, causing shade to pleat itself as drawn up.

Screw eye Screw with loop on end; installed on underside of mounting board for guiding shade cords.

Shade (lift) cord Small-diameter (.9- to 1.8-mm) braided polyester or nylon cord for rigging fabric shades.

Shirring tape Woven tape with one, two, or four heavy cords woven into construction; sewn to flat fabric, the cords gather fabric automatically when pulled.

Spring-tension rod Narrow metal rod with spring mechanism for inside-mount installations.

Twill tape Exceptionally strong tape with diagonal rib used for casings, ties, drawstrings, shade tapes, and decorative trims; available in variety of colors and widths (from $1/4$ inch to 1 inch).

Weight bar Metal rod or slat used for adding weight and stability to lower edge of fabric shade; $3/8$-inch brass rod recommended, but flat bar, wood dowel, curtain rod, or similar items also sometimes used.

Wood pole Round rod mounted to wall with special returns and angle irons; dowel screws are used to join pole and returns.

Decorative Trims

Band trim Wide variety of embroidered, beaded, sequined, fringed, or braided ribbons and trims finished on both edges.

Bias binding Prepackaged or custom-made fabric strips, usually cut on the bias to be used for casings, facings, and decorative trimming.

Braid Trim with three or more component strands plaited to form regular diagonal pattern along length.

Choux rosette Puffy, cabbage-shape rosette that encourages play of light and shade. (For details on how to create them, refer to Making a Choux Rosette on page 58.)

Cord Decorative twisted or braided cords that come with

or without lip (flange or tape): without lip, they can be sewn or glued as trim; with lip (called cord with lip or cord edge), they can be used as piping to accent and define edges.

Edging Narrow trimming, flat or ruffled, with one scalloped and one straight edge.

Eyelet Lightweight fabric in which holes have been cut and satin stitched to form decorative designs; available flat or ruffled and in variety of styles.

Fringe Decorative trim constructed of loose hanging strands of thread or yarn knotted and fastened to band or header; can be combined to add bulk or to customize color combinations. Styles include:

- Ball fringe or pom decor. Cut yarn ends fastened together to form ball, then hung from header by loop; can be used as purchased or combined to form lush decorative detail.
- Brush fringe or moss fringe. Lengths of cut yarn fastened together along one edge to create soft, thick, brushed edge; offered in variety of lengths and thicknesses.
- Bullion fringe. Tightly twisted yarn attached to header, creating spiraling or rope effect.
- Chainette fringe. Shimmering, cascading fringe usually made of rayon, silk, or polyester.
- Loop fringe. Similar to brush fringe, but with ends left uncut (looped).
- Swag fringe or rattail fringe. Decorative fringe with scalloped effect, often made of tubular rayon or silk cords attached to header.
- Tassel fringe. Tufts of cut yarn ends fastened together to form tassel, then attached to dangle from band or header.

Galloon Narrow lace or embroidery fabric with two scalloped edges.

Gimp Narrow trim made with tightly woven, tiny cord-like material, often forming loop or scroll design.

Lace Delicate open-work fabric made of threads woven together to form intricate, decorative designs; available in very narrow to very wide widths, from delicate sheers to heavy crochet-type weights.

Middy braid Narrow flat braid available in several widths.

Passementerie Generic French term for wide range of trimmings, including braid, gimp, fringe, tassels, metallic threads, and small glass beads.

Piping, welt, or welting Basic cording covered with fabric, designed for catching in a seam or creating a raised-edge accent.

Ribbon Woven fabric with cord finish or simple selvage along both edges, used for trimming and decoration; available in wide range of fibers and weaves and widths beginning at $\frac{1}{16}$ inch. Styles include:

- Grosgrain ribbon. Closely woven, corded, narrow fabric usually made of cotton, polyester, rayon, or silk; available in wide range of solids, as well as woven stripes and prints.
- Jacquard ribbon. Narrow fabric woven on jacquard loom capable of creating intricate designs; typical designs include multicolor florals, reversible patterns, and metallic-accented scroll or paisley designs.

Rickrack Decorative flat braid with uniform zigzag form; readily available prepackaged in wide range of colors and several widths from $\frac{1}{4}$-inch (baby) to $\frac{5}{8}$-inch (jumbo) and sometimes available in wider width by the yard.

Ruffling Strip of lace or fabric gathered into heading along one edge.

Soutache Very narrow, flat decorative braid woven in herringbone pattern with indentation at center for stitching.

Tassel Group of colored yarns bound together at top and hung as pendant ornament on draperies, valances, or tiebacks.

Tieback Narrow, straight, or shaped fabric band, braided cord, or metal holdback designed to pull back curtains and draperies to achieve most of view from window or provide decorative effect.

Twill tape Exceptionally strong tape with diagonal rib used for casings, ties, drawstrings, shade tapes, and decorative trims.

Woven bands Decorative trims, usually more than $1\frac{1}{2}$ inches wide, with two straight edges; may be woven on jacquard looms for intricate designs or on dobby looms for simple, often geometric designs.

Terms and Techniques

Austrian shade A softly ruched fabric shade usually made in a lightweight or sheer fabric.

Balloon shade A soft shade closely related to the Roman shade in construction, but using more fabric so that in the raised position, it bellows into soft poufs along the bottom edge.

Banding A strip of fabric folded under on one or both edges that is topstitched or fused to the face of the treatment.

Binding A method of finishing an edge with a fabric strip to prevent raveling and/or to serve as a decorative accent.

Casing/rod pocket A fabric tunnel created to allow a

weight rod curtain rod, drawstring, or elastic to be threaded through it.

Clean finish Techniques used to finish raw edges: zigzagging, serging, pinking, or encasing with fabric tape. Alternatively, specialty seams, such as French and flat fell, can be used to enclose the raw edges.

Cloud shade A cross between a Roman and a balloon shade; softer than a tailored Roman shade, but more tailored than a balloon shade.

Cut length Finished length of a treatment plus extra amount needed for hems, headers, and casings.

Cut width Finished width of a treatment with cut lengths seamed, and including allowances for side hems, seams, overlaps, and returns.

Drop Distance from the top of a treatment to the desired lower position.

Face fabric Decorator fabric used as primary fabric in a project.

Feed dog The "feet" on the sewing machine bed that feed the fabric under the presser foot. The feed dog can be lowered to prevent movement of the fabric and allow you to sew in one place.

Finished length Distance from the top edge to the bottom edge of a panel after it is sewn.

Finished width Size of a panel after it is sewn, including the face width, the return, and overlap.

Fullness Amount of fabric shirred or pleated into a treatment.

Gather/gathering Process of pulling up a given length of fabric to measure a smaller distance across, thereby creating soft, even pleats.

Header/heading Fabric extended above the casing, usually creating a ruff or ruffle once it is gathered up.

Inside mount Window treatment positioned just inside of the window frame; suitable only for windows with 1-inch or greater recess.

Miter/mitering Joining of two corner edges at an angle to create a neat finish.

Outside mount Window treatment positioned on window frame or on wall above and/or beyond frame.

Panel One or more widths of fabric sewn together.

Pleats
- Box. Flat-pressed symmetrical pleats with fabric folded back on both sides so adjoining side edges meet. Inverted pleats have the edges meeting on the right side of the panel.

- Goblet. Large cylindrical pleats pinched at the base to form goblet shapes.
- Pinch (also called French pleats). A triple pleat heading in which three folds of fabric are pinched together and tacked at the base.
- Soft. Pleats that begin as those above, but are hand tacked at the top edge of the heading only to create soft folds.

Projection Distance that the mounted rod or board extends from the wall.

Railroad To align pattern along the width of the fabric (horizontally) instead of along the length of the fabric (vertically). This method is usually used to eliminate or reduce seams or to follow a specific design line.

Repeat One complete pattern on a print or plaid fabric.

Return Portion of window treatment covering rod or board projection.

Roman shade A flat, tailored window shade that falls in graceful horizontal folds when raised and hangs flat when lowered.

Rosette Decoration created by arranging fabric to resemble a rose or an ornament suggesting a rose.

Selvage Tightly woven edge that runs along both sides of the length of fabric to prevent raveling.

Serging Using an overlock sewing machine that simultaneously stitches, trims, and overcasts a seam or raw edge.

Shirr Used interchangably with gather; also, to create a series of parallel rows of gathering.

Stitch in the ditch To stitch in the seam line on the right side of the project.

Stitches
- Backstitch. Reverse stitching to fasten threads at the beginning and end of a machine-stitched seam.
- Baste. A long, loose stitch by hand or machine, used to hold fabric layers together temporarily.
- Blind stitch. Sewing machine stitch consisting of four to six straight stitches, followed by one zigzag stitch; mocks the look of a hand-stitched hem.
- Edgestitch. Line of machine stitching $1/16$ inch from a seam line or edge.
- Hand tack. Stitch with repeated back-and-forth stiches in one place.
- Topstitching. Straight machine stitching, usually $1/8$ to $1/4$ inch from project edge and visible on the right side.

Width of fabric Distance from the left selvage edge to the right selvage edge of the fabric.

Resource Guide

Fabrics

B & J Fabric
263 West 40th Street
New York, NY 10018
(212) 354-8150
Pages 9, 30

Brunschwig & Fils
979 Third Avenue
New York, NY 10022
(212) 838-7878
Through architects and
interior designers.
Page 33

Calico Corners
203 Gale Lane
Kennett Square, PA 19348
(800) 821-7700, ext. 810
   for nearest retail outlet.
Large seller of decorative
fabrics, affordably priced.

Covington Fabric
15 East 26 Street
New York, NY 10010
(212) 689-2200
Page 34

Cowtan & Tout, Inc.
979 Third Avenue
New York, NY 10022
(212) 753-4488
Through architects and
interior designers.
Pages 10, 44

The Fabric Center
485 Electric Avenue
P.O. Box 8212
Fitchburg, MA 01420
(508) 343-4402
Mail-order source with
discounts on most major
decorative fabrics.

Hancock Fabrics
Mail Order Department
3841 Hinkleville Road
Paducah, KY 42001
(800) 845-8723, ext. 456
Mail-order source for
home decorating fabrics,
including mildew-resistant
fabrics. Also source for
sewing notions, regular and
transparent drapery tapes, and
Conso trims and home
decorating products.

Hinson & Co.
979 Third Avenue
New York, NY 10022
(212) 688-5538
Through architects and
interior designers.
Page 21

Pierre Deux
570 Madison Avenue
New York, NY 10021
(212) 570-9343
Pages 57, 58

Waverly
79 Madison Avenue
New York, NY 10016
(800) 423-5881
Through architects and
interior designers and select
retail stores.
Page 19

Drapery Rods and Hardware

Country Curtains
At the Red Lion Inn
Stockbridge, MA 01262
(800) 224-6020
Mail-order source
for curtains and drapery
rods and hardware.

General Clutch Corp.
200 Harvard Avenue
Stamford, CT 06902
(800) 552-5100
Manufacturer of
"Rollease," a made-to-
order shade lift system
for Roman, balloon,
and Austrian shades.

**Graber/Springs
   Window Fashions***
7549 Graber Road
Middleton, WI 53562
(800) 356-9102
Major manufacturer of
drapery rods and hardware.

Kirsch*
PO Box 0370
Sturgis, MI 49091
(800) 528-1407
Mail-order source for lace
curtains and drapery rods,
hardware, and keyhole
support brackets.

Rue de France
78 Thames Street
Newport, RI 02840
(800) 777-0998
Mail-order source
for lace curtains and drapery
rods and hardware.

**Warm Window
   Products Inc.**
16120 Woodinville-
   Redmond Road, #5
Woodinville, MA 98072
(800) 234-9276
Window insulation fabric/
system. Does not sell retail;
call for dealer referrals.

Trims and Notions

Clotilde, Inc.
2 Sew Smart Way
B8031
Stevens Point, WI 54481
(800) 772-2891
Mail-order source for sewing
notions, including Perfect
Pleater™.

Conso Products*
PO Box 326
Union, SC 29379
(800) 845-2431
Major manufacturer
of trims, drapery tapes,
and other home decorating
and sewing notions, including
the Claesson selection of
traditional and unique
drapery hardware.

Hollywood Trims*
Prym-Dritz Corporation
PO Box 5028
Spartanburg, SC 29304
(800) 845-4948
Major manufacturer of trims.
Page 19

M&J Trimming
1014 Sixth Avenue
New York, NY 10018
(212) 391-8731
Retail store and mail-order
source for decorative
trimming.
Pages 26, 78, 82

**These resources do not sell
directly to the public, but you
may contact them for the store
or source nearest you.**

Nancy's Notions
PO Box 683
Beaver Dam, WI 53916
Mail-order source for sewing
notions, including regular and
transparent drapery tapes and
wide-width decorator fabrics.

National Thread &
Supply Corp.
695 Red Oak Road
Stockbridge, GA 30281
(800) 331-7600,
    ext. A-219
Mail-order source for sewing
notions, Kirsch rods, regular
and transparent drapery tapes,
hook-and-loop tapes, fabric
dressing, and many other
home decorating supplies.

C.M. Offray & Son,
Inc.*
Route 24, Box 601
Chester, NJ 07930-0601
(908) 879-4700
Major source for ribbons
and ribbon trims.
Pages 19, 40

Designers

Laura Ashley
714 Madison Avenue
New York, NY 10021
(212) 735-5009
Page 76

Brett Design, Inc.
350 East 79th Street
New York, NY 10021
(212) 744-6601
Page 16

George Constant, Inc.
425 East 63rd Street
New York, NY 10021
(212) 751-1907
Pages 59, 73

Edmond De Rocker
Associates
56 Glen Street
Glen Falls, NY 12801
(518) 792-6555
Page 70

Billy W. Francis
Francis Russell Design
Decoration, Inc.
964 Third Avenue
New York, NY 10155
(212) 980-4151
Pages 50, 54

Glenn Gissler
Design, Inc.
174 Fifth Avenue, #402
New York, NY 10010
(212) 727-3220
Pages 5, 40

Greenbaum Interiors
Mt. Kemble Avenue
Morristown, NJ 07960
(201) 425-5500
Page 64

Mark Hampton
654 Madison Avenue
New York, NY 10021
(212) 753-4110
Page 69

Irvine and Fleming
150 East 58th Street
New York, NY 10022
(212) 888-6000
Pages 67, 69

Donna Lang Ltd
180 Main Street
Chatham, NJ 07928
(201) 635-4085
Pages 9, 10, 30, 33, 44,
88–89

Michael LaRocco Ltd.
150 East 58th Street
New York, NY 10022
(212) 755-5588
Page 53

Paul Leonard
P.O. Box 258
Washington, CT 06794
(203) 868-2338
Page 47

Lincoln Interiors Inc.
4 Birch Street
Locust Valley, NY 11560
(516) 759-6100
Page 48

Tonin MacCallum
21 East 90th Street
New York, NY 10128
(212) 831-8909
Page 62

Carl Steele, Inc.
1606 Pine Street
Philadelphia, PA 19103
(215) 546-5530
Page 75

Stebbins & Co.
79 East Putnam Avenue
Greenwich, CT 06830
(203) 661-0066
Cover and page 61

Robert E. Tartarini
Interiors
PO Box 293
Old Westbury, NY 11568
(516) 338-0257
Page 27

Gerald C. Tolomeo, Ltd.
Design and
Decoration
96 Rockland Avenue
W. Paterson, NJ 07424
(201) 487-1006
(212) 768-1660
Page 21

David Webster
254 West 25th Street
New York, NY 10001
(212) 924-8932
Pages 2, 66

Bennett and Judie
Weinstock Interiors,
Inc.
2026 Delancey Place
Philadelphia, PA 19103
(215) 735-2026

Gail Whiting Design
Consultants
Route 202 North
Bedminster, NJ 07921
(908) 781-2092
Pages 1, 12, 39

Vicente Wolf
333 West 39th Street
New York, NY 10018
(212) 465-0590
Page 37

Workrooms

Angela Corizzi
31 Sixth Avenue
Clifton, NJ 07011
(201) 772-5330
Page 21

Judith A. Petersen
Enterprises
19 Sherman Avenue
Summit, NJ 07901
(908) 277-3994
Page 10, 44, 57

Stessl & Neugebauer
9 Industrial Place
Summit, NJ 07901
(908) 277-3340
Through architects and
interior designers.
Pages 9, 30, 88–89

Index

Aesthetics, 11, 14
Angle irons, 81, 90
Attachments, 25–26
Austrian shades, 51–53, 92
  aesthetics, 14
  basics, 52–53
  checklist, 15
  cords, 53
  mounting and rigging,
    22–26, 53
  placement, 28
  sewing, 21, 72–73
  sheer, 72–73
  shirred, 53, 73
  tape for, 53, 90
  yardage, 52, 72

Balloon shades, 51–71,
  74–77, 92
  basics, 52–53
  casual, 66
  checklist, 15
  cloud, 59, 60, 67–68, 93
  cords, 60
  festoon, 76–77
  hems, 52
  lining, 17
  mounting and rigging, 22–26,
    53, 55
  placement, 28
  pleated, 67–68, 70–71, 74–75
  rings, 75, 77
  rosette, 56
  ruffled, 63, 64–65
  sewing, 21, 54–55, 56, 59, 60,
    63–68, 70–71, 74–75, 77
  with shirring, 54–55
  trim, 75
  yardage, 52, 54, 56, 59, 60,
    63, 64, 67, 70, 74, 76–77
Band trims, 18, 91, 92
Bias, 84–86, 90
Binding, 84–85, 91, 92

Care and cleaning. *See*
  Maintenance
Cloud shades, 8, 93
  box-pleated, 67–68
  with cord, 60
  sheer, 59
Cords, 18, 91–92
  for Austrian shades, 53
  for balloon shades, 53, 60
  danger of, 25
  finishing, 83
  for rigging, 26
  for Roman shades, 42–45
Cornices, 80–81, 91
Cost factors, 15, 17
Cotton, 20, 88, 89
Curtain rods, 26, 91
Cut length, 29, 93

Design details, 29

Dressing, 33, 53, 91
Drop, 93

Edging, 92
Energy efficiency, 15, 32

Fabric, 92, 93
  for Austrian and balloon
    shades, 52
  choosing, 17, 32
  cleaning, 17
  glossary, 88–90
  measuring and estimating, 27
  for Roman shades, 32
  yardage calculation, 28–29, 34
  See also specific fabrics
Fasteners, 25–26, 91
Fiber
  care, 20
  glossary, 88–90
  natural, 17
  See also specific fibers
Flush method, 83
Fringe, 18, 92

Gathering, 93
Glue, 92
Grommets, 42–45, 91

Hardware, 90–91
  for Austrian and balloon
    shades, 53
  checklist, 25
  installing, 23, 25
  for Roman shades, 33
Hems, 32–33, 44, 52
Hook-and-loop fasteners,
  25–26, 91

Interlining, 17, 32, 89

Knotting, 60

Length measurements, 22, 93
Light control, 13, 15, 17
Linen, 20, 88, 89
Lining, 89
  for Austrian and balloon
    shades, 52
  fabric for, 17
  for Roman shades, 32, 44–45

Magnetic side rails, 32
Maintenance, 14, 17, 33, 53
Marking, 21
Measurements, 27
  for Austrian and balloon
    shades, 52
  length, 22, 93
  for Roman shades, 32
  width, 22, 93
Mitering, 35, 93
Motifs, 29
Mounting, 22–26

Austrian and balloon shades,
  53, 73
  inside, 22, 27, 91, 93
  outside, 22, 27, 93
  Roman shades, 33, 43, 49
  techniques, 80–81
Mounting board, 63, 81, 82, 91

Notions, 25, 90–91
Nylon, 20, 89

Panels, 8, 93
Passementerie, 92
Patterns, 17, 29
  see also Print fabric
Piping, 86, 92
Pleats, 93
  for balloon shades, 56, 67–68,
    70–71, 74–75
  for Roman shades, 48–49
Poles, 64–65, 81, 91
Polyester, 20, 89
Poufed hems, 52
Print fabric
  border, 88
  measuring and estimating, 27
  repeats, 29
  yardage calculation, 28, 29
  See also Patterns
Privacy, 13, 15
Projection, 93

Repeats, 29, 93
Returns, 25, 93
Ribbon, 92
Rickrack, 92
Rigging, 22–25, 26
  Austrian and balloon shades, 73
  Roman shades, 43, 49
Ring tape, 21, 23, 90
Rings, 21, 23
  for balloon shades, 75, 77
  for Roman shades, 34–35, 36,
    45, 46
Rods, 26, 91
Roman shades, 8, 31–47, 93
  aesthetics, 14
  banded, 38
  basics, 32–33
  checklist, 15
  grommet and cord, 42–45
  hems, 32–33, 44
  hobbled, 48–49
  lined, 17, 44–45
  measuring and estimating, 27
  mounting and rigging, 21–26,
    43, 49
  placement, 28
  rings, 34–35, 36, 45, 46
  sewing, 21, 34–36, 38, 39,
    41–43, 45, 46
  sheer, 36
  simple, 34–35
  stationary, 39

tied-up, 41
trim, 18
unlined, 44, 46
yardage, 32, 34, 36, 38, 39,
  41, 42, 44, 46, 48
Room function, 14
Rosettes, 56, 58, 91, 93
Ruffling, 63, 64–65, 92

Scallops, 53, 54
Seaming, 17
Selvage, 93
Serging, 93
Sewing, 21
  Austrian shades, 21, 72–73
  balloon shades, 21, 54–56, 60,
    63–68, 70–71, 74–75, 77
  Roman shades, 21, 34–36, 38,
    39, 41–43, 45, 46
Shirring, 53, 54–55, 73, 91, 93
Silk, 20, 88, 90
Soutache, 92
Stapled attachment, 25
Stitches, 93
Studs, 24
Stuffing, 53
Style, 13

Tape, 21, 90, 91, 92
  applying, 23
  for Austrian shades, 53
  hook-and-loop, 25–26
Tassel, 92
Temperature control, 13
Tieback, 92
Trim, 18, 83–87
  applying, 82
  bias, 84–86
  finishing ends, 83
  flat, 35
  glossary, 91–92
  piping, 86
  pleated, 75
  yardage, 29

Unravel and tack method, 83
Upholstered cornice, 80–81

Valences, 41

Wall fasteners, 23, 91
Weight bar, 32, 36, 52, 91
Width measurements, 22, 93
Window dressings, 13–15
Wool, 20, 90

Yardage, 28–29
  for Austrian shades, 52, 72
  for balloon shades, 52, 54, 56,
    59, 60, 63, 64, 66, 67, 70,
    74, 76–77
  for bias, 84
  for Roman shades, 32, 34, 36,
    38, 39, 41, 42, 44, 46, 48